THE CONSUMER'S ELECTRIC CAR

ERNEST H. WAKEFIELD, PhD

ANN ARBOR SCIENCE
PUBLISHERS INC
P.O. BOX 1425 • ANN ARBOR, MICH. 48106

Published by ANN ARBOR SCIENCE PUBLISHERS, Inc.
230 Collingwood, P. O. Box 1425, Ann Arbor, Michigan 48106

Copyright © 1977 by Ernest H. Wakefield
1927 Sherman Avenue, Evanston, Illinois 60201

Library of Congress Catalog Card No. 76-050984
ISBN   0-250-40155-X

"It is impossible for a man who takes a survey of what is already known, not to see what an immensity in every branch of science yet remains to be discovered. . . . I join you therefore in branding as cowardly the idea that the human mind is incapable of further advances."

Thomas Jefferson
Letter to a Student
Monticello, June 18, 1799

Dedicated to
H. H. Higbie
Professor of Electrical Engineering
University of Michigan

FOREWORD—BY A CONSUMER

I am a consumer. And heaven knows I need guidance. Increasingly these days, while hydrocarboning down the road, I worry about the future. There I am, blithely burning the sunlight it took nature 40 million years to store. When that's all gone—and it will be all gone make no doubt of it—where will I, poor Mr. Consumer, be, in my gasoline-powered vehicle?

Where I'll be is in one of Dr. Wakefield's remarkable electric cars. *The Consumer's Electric Car* is a book about the future; and it seems to be a future that has already arrived. Dr. Wakefield is driving his electric car cheerfully around America, successfully importuning receptacles for charging his vehicle when the need arises. Many other drivers in their merry electric cars apparently are doing the same. Ladies and gentlemen, put down my name as well on your list of electric car recruits.

When I read this book, I knew about electric cars only what Tom Swift had taught me. After reading the book, I modestly consider myself astonishingly well informed. This book, though not lengthy, is as compact as the battery of an electric; and it supplies a comprehensive guide to the electric vehicle, what it is, the technical advancements that have brought it to the present, how it works, and why. I have been driving a gasoline-powered whatchacallit for years, and the truth is that thanks to Dr. Wakefield's book, I know considerably more about the electric car than I do about its gasguzzling old internal-combustion uncle. Goodbye, uncle.

It amazes me to reflect that I really understand the workings of an electric car—I who never before fully understood the workings of any car. I have a genial confidence that I could drive an electric, accomplish basic troubleshooting, charge it up, and continually enjoy that little ego-dividend of knowing what is happening when I start it up. All of this is thanks to the clarity and completeness of Dr. Wakefield's presentation. Believe it or not, I *even* know what it means if on acceleration I hear water squirting from the cell breather orifice. Before reading this book, I could never have explained with any degree of confidence what the dickens a cell breather orifice is. Now I could, and what is more I know what to do if it squirts!

The Consumer's Electric Car is technically thorough, impeccably scientific, and vigorously detailed. Yet above and beyond these, it is a passionate retelling of a love affair that is still going on. Dr. Wakefield is positively passionate about these electric buggies of his, and the reader quite early has a strong, strange feeling that he could easily share that passion, given an opportunity. And Dr. Wakefield assures him in the very first sentence that his future may very well contain an electric car. I hope so, and I express that hope as an enlightened tribute to the information in this book.

What strikes me about Dr. Wakefield's electric car is that it is first and foremost a civilized machine, realistically designed for the modern needs of urban and suburban dwellers. Each morning I drive my IC (Internal Combustion) Javelin, or whatever name it has, about two miles to work, and reverse course in the evening. During the trip, if traffic is light, and I really feel audacious, my top speed may get up to 35 mph. Two-thirds of the energy in that automobile is wasted. Out the pipe it goes to tickle and torment the lungs of myself and others. The electric car does not pollute, it wastes far less energy, and provides just the power I need for normal runabout activities. Electric Car, where have you been all my driving life? No matter, now you've come; let me give you a charge and we'll drive away together, leaving no nasty particulates in the air.

Civilized is the word for the electric car, not only because it is environmentally clean, but also because it conveys the impression of friendliness and serenity. Actually, my conscience whispers that I should walk to work each day, but prudence shouts that if I do on that busy thoroughfare, one of those IC furies will pancake me permanently into the freeway. No thanks. But electric cars sound far less furious and lethal. They offer efficient transportation, yet still they proceed with civility and show compassion for lovers, joggers, bicyclists and walkers.

I agree with Dr. Wakefield that there probably will be an electric car in my future—and yours. When that happens, both you and I will find ourselves frequently referring to this book to check our facts and refresh our memories about what to do when smoke comes from the battery compartment. Or we'll want to study through the mathematics of electric vehicle efficiency again in order to convince a friend that he too should "go electric," or a thousand other electric vehicle points we want to keep in mind.

Right now, before that first electric car arrives in our garage, this is a curious, fun and intriguing book to read. Dr. Wakefield covers his subject so lucidly, most nonmathematicians can grasp and apply the formulae in the analytical sections without hair-tearing effort. The author's expertise shines through with enormous accuracy on every page, and with a sly, persistent wit that makes the book a pleasure to read even by roller skate enthusiasts with no present plans for competitive modes of transport.

Surprisingly, the book also provides a running commentary on the history of automotive and electric technology that most readers will find interesting and welcome. This is offered virtually as an aside. It is a special bonus in the book, and my hunch is that the historical facts appear largely because they happened to be present in the author's busy head, and he simply shared them with us as he explained in detail each element of the electric car. I don't know what others may claim, but as for myself, let it be stated that I was both startled and delighted to learn what Gaston Plate in 1859 may have done with his wife's petticoat! Suffice it to say that the modern electric car—and much more—apparently owe a considerable debt to that petticoat. (Suggestion: When reading this book, don't, I repeat don't neglect the foot-notes. You'll thank me for the tip.) Incidentally, let it also be stated that I was startled, delighted, and remarkably informed by *The Consumer's Electric Car.* I predict that many other readers will feel the same—and that most of us one of these years will be doing precisely what Dr. Wakefield wants us to do and thinks we should—driving electric cars.

Roy Meador
Ann Arbor, Michigan

PREFACE

The purpose of this book is to help the consumer understand electric cars since his future probably will contain one. The over-the-road electric vehicle is a concept that is still controversial in the popular mind, and it tends to evoke flat assertions from almost any observer. Yet relatively few persons have actually driven modern, high-performance electric vehicles. On the other hand, those few dozen specialists who are deeply engaged in electric vehicle design recognize this alternate type of transportation as a challenge of commanding importance to contemporary mankind.

In the United States, as in other industrial nations, there is a growing effort directed toward developing more effective electric vehicles and fabricating batteries with greater energy storage per unit of weight. Not fully appreciated at present is the fact that the best battery-equipped electric vehicles are already adequate for many urban tasks. At this writing, the well-designed electric vehicle can be shown to have the same cost per mile over its life span as does a subcompact car. Moreover, electrics can be designed to achieve speeds and accelerations equal to those of internal combustion vehicles. Electrics yield only in range.

Being built in small quantities, electrics can be constructed of corrosion-proof materials to provide a far longer life. The most suitable areas for electric car use at present are urban centers, and to achieve optimum results, electrics should be used for particular tasks. They do not possess the universality of the gasoline-powered vehicle. The electric, with an on-board charger, after a trip should have its charging cord connected to a convenient outlet, and the battery rejuvenated for the vehicle's next excursion. This procedure will maximize the daily effective range, which in a 10-hour period can now approach 100 miles of urban driving.

This figure comes into perspective when it is realized that 50% of the gasoline-powered cars in America travel less than 28 miles per day, and that 54% of the trips are under 5 miles. Such usage is already efficiently attainable by the better electric cars.

When one is constantly involved with electric vehicles, a certain sensitivity to their use is gained. The author of this book routinely drives a high-performance electric vehicle. He has been intimately concerned with their conception, design, manufacture, marketing, maintenance and chronicling for many years of his life. In addition, he has taught electrical engineering and manufactured complex electronic apparatus.

This book provides a comprehensive introduction to modern electric vehicles. A brief section covers basic electricity. Then the elements of an electric vehicle are described together with their method of operation. Always the care of these elements is stressed. Basing his information on many years experience driving electric vehicles, the author provides a section containing helpful hints from the road, followed by novel and speculative ideas that have been presented to him concerning these vehicles.

The serious engineer engaged in developing electric cars is a natural target for many concepts related to their design. This book includes line drawings illustrating principles that are widely repeated. Some of these casually related ideas are Utopian, while others have merit. There is no reason why a person should not dream, whatever the idea. All of us in our make-up contain both the goose and the owl. In modern technology the line of separation between the wild and the wise can often be narrow. For progress in electric vehicles, the educated, disciplined mind appears best equipped, yet like the "sport" in nature, the unexpected can happen.

Included in the book are various schemes of perpetual motion, the utilization of solar energy, applying the power of the wind, the application of rolling resistance to enhance motive power, and some schemes that are even more obscure.

Electric vehicles in many places can be seen performing well on the streets. The writer, after many years of intimate familiarity with both electric and internal combustion vehicles, sees a market gradually opening for electrics. He recognizes that IC vehicles will be dominant for many years in personal transportation, barring unanticipated developments. It is also believed that for long-distance road trucking, the self-contained electric energy source as an alternate to petroleum fuel has yet to be conceived. But the reader desiring a rewarding new experience should begin driving a modern high-performance electric vehicle regularly in and around his community.

Writing this book for 1977 publication, the author was faced with a choice between metric or English measurements. To assure that the text is clearly understood, and in consideration of the fact that much of the material will be new to readers, it was decided to use mensuration and units with which the general, well-informed reader is now accustomed.

Ernest H. Wakefield
Evanston, Illinois

ACKNOWLEDGMENTS

While writing, the author has benefited from echoes in his mind repeating thousands of conversations on electric vehicles with his peers, with electric utility personnel in all sections of the U.S., with automobile dealers, with engineers and executives in England, Continental Europe, the Soviet Union, Australia and Asia. Scientists and technicians around the world have given the author a gracious reception and generous help.

The author is particularly indebted to those below who have read the manuscript in preliminary form and have improved on it. Included are Dr. Gordon J. Murphy, Professor of Electrical Engineering, Northwestern University; Roy Meador, Science Writer, Ann Arbor, Michigan; Paul M. Martin, Chairman of the DC Motor Group of the Motor and Generator Section of the National Electric Manufacturers Association; Dr. James T. Waber, Professor of Materials Science, Northwestern University; and William H. Shafer, Section Engineer, Commonwealth Edison Company. Richard B. Pratt, Vice President, Continental Car Distributors, Inc., has offered timely suggestions to help keep in focus the reader to whom the book is directed.

The author is most appreciative of the cooperation of the publishers and manufacturers who graciously gave their permission to use various illustrations in this book.

Ernest H. Wakefield

CONTENTS

CHAPTER 1

ELEMENTS OF ELECTRIC VEHICLES

"The motor car is, more than any other object, the expression of the nation's character and the nation's dream."

E. B. White, "One Man's Meat," *Motor Cars,* 1940

Electricity and its handmaiden magnetism were present when the earth was formed, and they will still be present when the planet is consumed by the sun. Long before that final moment, electricity may be one of the tools some men use to seek further habitation elsewhere in space. Electricity at times crashes high in the heavens, and magnetism appears from the bowels of the earth.

Great forces are present in each; and when one is possessed, the other also is at hand. Electricity measures the quick, it is absent from the dead. This book explores in detail the immediate and future application of electricity to solve the challenge of human transportation.

Transportation is an engaging subject, one that has always attracted the interest and efforts of man. Efficiently transporting himself and his possessions is one of man's enduring obsessions and never-ending quests. The history of human progress can be logically recounted in terms of transportation strides, from primitive to modern methods. Is the electric vehicle going to be the next step forward in this historic progress? At this instant, where do we stand with electric personal transportation?

The term electric* vehicles is a broad one. It encompasses on-the-road, off-the-road, in-plant, dual-mode, and mass transit electric vehicles, as well

---

*William Gilbert, Court Physician to Queen Elizabeth I, was the first (1600) to use the word *electric*, which he derived from the Greek word for amber, *elektron.* He was also the first to postulate that the earth was a giant magnet and applied this concept for the observed action of a magnetic compass. He has been honored in the application of his name: 1 gilbert = $10/4\pi$ ampere-turns.

1

as a miscellaneous class. Each of these headings is further classified into subheadings. This book concerns itself primarily with the class known as consumers' electric vehicles. This class is chiefly designed for personal transportation. The operational speed and acceleration characteristics of these vehicles parallel the performance of more conventional internal combustion (IC) vehicles. Only in range do they compare modestly with IC performance. These high-performance electric vehicles are sufficiently powered to provide speeds on demand up to 60 mph, sufficient for expressway travel. While much of this book is applicable to all electric vehicles, its main thrust is directed toward high-performance consumers' electric vehicles.

Minimum requirements for a consumer's electric vehicle include a chassis, body, battery, magnetic contactor, control circuit and a motor. A charger for the battery may be aboard or separate. The chassis and body may be converted from an IC vehicle, or they may be initially designed for an electric vehicle. This discussion will be limited to those elements peculiar to electric vehicles, and will serve as an introduction for more complete studies of individual elements. Space will not be devoted to the vehicle itself, the chassis or the body. Many manuals adequately describe the conventional automobile and its construction.

DESIGN CONSIDERATIONS

In the elevated states of electric vehicle design, the course often taken seems to parallel the imaginative plots of poetry and drama: Dilemma within dilemma, solution and countersolution, success and failure, true paths and false, satisfaction and dissatisfaction, compromise and no compromise, copper for current, iron for flux, weight and power, lightness and acceleration, sale and nonsale, cost and expense. Innumerable factors must be juggled, and the total forms a reality too intricate for belief, but that cannot be doubted. A designer must contend with labyrinthine possibilities and needs, while pursuing his task with persistence and inspired passion. He needs to be a computer-minded Canute. Only then will the ultimate consumer be well rewarded and receive full value. The importance of the designer's work cannot be exaggerated. His efforts can be the fountainhead reflecting the best that a nation offers.

How are the challenges of design best confronted in connection with electric vehicles? An electric vehicle is a type of transportation for specialized applications. It may be for personal travel or for the transfer of goods. In general, the configuration of the body determines the vehicle's use. Both categories, however, will involve the elements listed above. In the design of an electric vehicle, one first determines its use. If it must travel on expressways, it should have characteristics that enable it to merge and flow with the traffic. If the vehicle will be used only on secondary roads, its specifications may be more modest. Whatever its use, it should be well engineered for safety, performance, comfort and ease of maintenance.

Below are described in more detail the specific elements of high-performance electric vehicles. Figures 1 through 5 show actual production models.

Figure 1. Electric GameTime 120, also available as Roadster with rollbar and windshield. Top speed 60 mph. Acceleration 0-30 mph in eight sec. Single-charge range in urban driving 60-70 miles. Ten-hour range 100 miles. Energy used per mile is equivalent to 123 mi/gal. Courtesy Su Kemper.

An electric vehicle should be designed as a total system. The mass of the vehicle, its load-carrying ability, its desired acceleration, its top speed, the range desired—all these criteria will serve to determine the capacity, voltage and quality of the battery, the size cabling required, the type of control system, the torque speed curve of the motor, the characteristics of the transmission and the differential. Too many vehicles in the past have simply been assembled with little regard for grace in design or the intended application of the final user. These vehicles have functioned, but they have neither advanced the art nor won friends and converts. A carefully designed electric vehicle wins plaudits from each person who drives or inspects it. The charger,

Figure 2. The Woody 120 seats two plus suitcases. Top speed 60 mph. Acceleration 0-30 mph in eight sec. Single-charge range in urban driving 60-70 miles. Ten-hour range: 100 miles. Courtesy M. D. Williams

Figure 3. The motive power battery, riding a pallet, may be readily withdrawn for servicing. Courtesy Su Kemper.

Figure 4. The Linear Alpha, "Seneca." Top speed 57 mph. Acceleration 0-30 mph in eight sec. Single-charge range in urban driving 35 miles. Ten-hour range: 70-80 miles. Seneca and Thunderbolt 240 are the same car.
Courtesy Commonwealth Edison Company.

Figure 5. The "Seneca." The charging device, specially designed motor, and electronic controller are visible under the hood. Courtesy Linear Alpha, Inc.

if placed aboard the vehicle, the batteries, the controller and the motor have substantial weight. Thus, care must be exercised in determining their ideal location. The final product must be safe and handle well at all designed speeds. To achieve desired results, the location and linkage both mechanically and electrically of all elements involve critical choices.

When a person drives a modern electric vehicle (as illustrated), he inserts the ignition key as usual. What happens? Unlike an internal combustion car, as long as the electric car is at rest, the electric motor need not be in operation. When he wishes to move forward, the driver engages the clutch pedal and with the transmission stick selects his starting gear. He depresses the accelerator to the speed he intends to use in advancing. Reaching his chosen speed, the operator lets up on the accelerator pedal naturally and drives as he normally would. To stop, he removes his foot from the accelerator pedal and brakes the car. His foot should always be free from the clutch pedal. On renewed acceleration, because of the natural high starting torque of the motor, he may start forward in the gear at which he was driving without reference to either the clutch or stick shift. He follows this same procedure when reversing the car, except that after turning on the ignition key, the driver selects the "reverse" position for the transmission stick. The reader quickly perceives that driving a modern electric vehicle is remarkably similar to driving a gasoline-powered car.

Because electric cars for many years will be the second or even the third car in a family, modern electric vehicles are expected to maintain a certain austerity, a modest size, and a relatively low curb weight. Such discipline stretches the vehicle's range on a single charge. As these vehicles are to be used essentially for local transportation, the driver will be aboard his car probably less than 30 minutes, and more typically less than 10 minutes as seen below.

To obtain a handle on trip length, the Federal Highway Administration made an extensive study in 1969 on driving habits of the American people. As a result of this inquiry, Table I could be constructed. It tabulates the

Table I. Distributions of Automobile Trips

Trip Length (one-way miles)	Percent of Annual Trips	Percent of Annual Vehicle Miles
Under 5	54.1	11.1
5-9	19.6	13.8
10-15	13.8	18.7
16-20	4.3	9.1
21-30	4.0	11.8
31-40	1.6	6.6
41-50	0.8	4.3
51-99	1.0	7.6
100 and over	0.8	17.0
Total	100.0	100.0

Courtesy H. J. Schwartz.
Source: U.S. Department of Transportation/Federal Highway Administration.[1]

distribution of automobile travel in discrete increments. While some time has elapsed since that study, the distribution is still considered representative, although average annual miles traveled per year has historically been creeping upward, being 10,184 miles in 1972.[2]

If one takes this figure and divides by the number of days in the year, the daily figure is 27.9 miles. In a study of driving habits in Los Angeles, half the people in this independent examination traveled less than 28.2 miles per day.[3] Both figures appear to agree and represent all classes of vehicles: first car, second car, and third car in a family. But as Harvey J. Schwartz relates concerning these figures, "The design of an electric vehicle cannot simply meet the average requirement of the user, but must instead meet his real, or more importantly, his perceived needs."[4]

Schwartz then, with the aid of a computer, applied the Monte Carlo Simulation technique, a concept believed first used in nuclear physics, to convert annual averages into daily driving patterns, and he developed Figure 6, "the simulation of daily usefulness as a function of daily range."

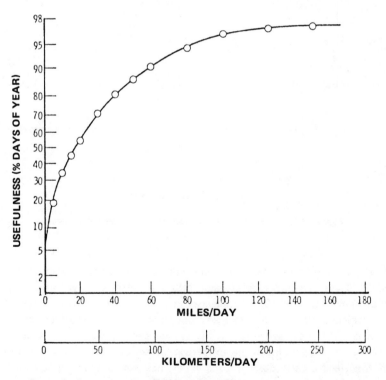
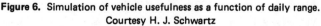

Figure 6. Simulation of vehicle usefulness as a function of daily range.
Courtesy H. J. Schwartz

And in Figure 7, he applies this calculation to average annual mileage. Referring to Figure 6, if one said that to satisfy a driver the electric vehicle must be available for 95% of the trips to be made, the car would need a range of 82 miles per day of urban driving. This range at present seems unlikely. But if one studies Figure 7, as annual travel is decreased, less daily range is required to achieve the 95% satisfaction condition.

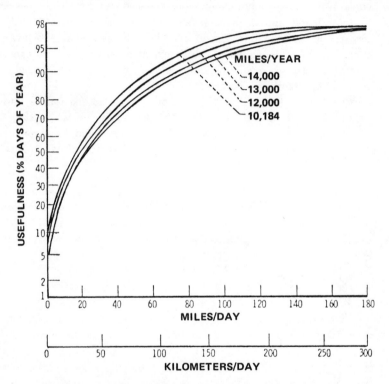

Figure 7. Sensitivity of simulation results to average annual mileage.
Courtesy H. J. Schwartz

The author himself has driven an electric vehicle for more than eight years and believes that in the foreseeable future the average driver will be content with much less than 10,000 miles per year in his electric vehicle. The electric vehicle should be used as a second car, and is not, as the Schwartz study implies, used in the same way as the average car. Just as it would be a mistake to consider a dune buggy an average car, so it would be an error to think of the electric car. Based on his experience, rather than supposition, the author thinks that in the 1970s and 1980s, the annual average miles for electric vehicles will be in the 3000-6000 miles per year class. This is comparable to the mileage many families put on their second car. Let the reader follow his own experience in this matter.

With this more realistic lower figure, and interpolating on Figure 7, one obtains 40-60 miles per day as the range satisfactory to 95% of car drivers. These values are well within the single-charge range of the GameTime 120, the Woody 120 classes of electric vehicles, and even of the Thunderbolt 240 conversion classes of vehicles, if charging is done during the day.

The kernel of the Schwartz study is to demonstrate that the emphasis on battery research should be directed toward the intermediate battery, which will take a vehicle 80-100 miles on a single charge, rather than on the far-term battery, which could power an electric vehicle over 150 miles. Herein Schwartz sounds a warning.

Opting to satisfy present needs, Hamilton, cited above, writes concerning Los Angeles, "as a secondary car in a two-car household (a 54-mile-range car) could be adequate on over 97% of driving days."

Both Schwartz and Hamilton record the results of IC vehicle driving patterns. It is expected that the advent of the electric car will subtly introduce an ameliorating and moderating influence on such patterns. Marketing men already know and scholars will discover that the psychology of the driver/ buyer is a constantly changing enigma, requiring tireless study to anticipate. Hence, the proliferation of automobile styles and models. What will satisfy him next? The suppliers of future automobiles can never stop seeking the answer to that question.

At this time, those interested in encouraging the use of electric vehicles, for whatever reason, should aim at that segment of the market that electric vehicles especially fit, and at that group of drivers who for their own reasons want to own one. In every town, city and hamlet, there are always those refreshing souls, the innovators, of whom Thoreau wrote, "If a man does not keep pace with his companions, perhaps it is because he hears a different drummer. Let him step to the music which he hears, however measured or far away."[5] The "music" of electric vehicles will appeal to a few in every community, and that few will be the vanguard leading to the many.

ELECTRIC PASSENGER VEHICLES

Electric-powered sedans can be designed to carry 2-4 people. Since present cars commute with a statistical average of 1.3 persons[6] per trip, and since electric vehicles by their very nature are second or third cars in a family (eschewing the movement of kith and kin from one city to the next), the development of both two- and four-passenger electric cars can be positively argued. Yet the first funding by the federal government was for four passenger vehicles, a size that may be in the minority in the future. While living almost a decade with modern electric vehicles, the writer has experienced difficulty in breaking the chains of the immediate past. Diversity clearly is desirable. There are indications that electric vehicles when they arrive will come in their own distinctive garb and will be readily identifiable as "electrics." One reason for preparing this volume is to assist the consumer with his buying power in encouraging the emergence of creditable, well-engineered electric vehicles.

The GameTime 120 automobile is a good example of a high-performance electric vehicle, offering a curb weight with charger of 1660 pounds, a battery to curb weight ratio of 47%, and a low drag coefficient due to its excellent aerodynamics. The vehicle is powered to deliver a top speed of 60 mph. Its acceleration from 0-30 mph is eight seconds. The vehicle has an urban driving range of some 60 miles. Its energy consumption is 0.3 kilowatt-hour per mile, as measured at the mains. This number is equivalent to a gasoline mileage of 123 miles per gallon.* There is a 120-volt on-board charger. The battery, if reenergized nightly, and recharged while the vehicle is parked during the day, will yield an urban driving range of 100 miles in a ten-hour day. It is thought that characteristics of commercial electric vehicles will not greatly exceed these figures until well into the 1980s.

The GameTime 120 is also available as a roadster model, equipped with a safety roll-bar and windshield, with a closure for the area in between.

The Woody 120 bears the same fabricated aluminum chassis as the Game-Time 120. This chassis consists of a tube with a rectangular cross-section, in which the motive power battery slides on a convenient pallet. In both vehicles, when the batteries require servicing, they are withdrawn from the front of the vehicle onto a low dolly as shown in Figure 3. With the development of an infrastructure for electric vehicles, service station personnel, when batteries are low, might withdraw the depleted set and insert a newly charged group as shown in Figure 3. The driver would pay a fixed charge for this service just as he now purchases gasoline. Such a concept is sketched in Chapter 6.

A good example of converting high-production vehicles is the Thunberbolt 240 wagon, also available as the Runabout. In this vehicle, the on-board charger is under the front hood. The motive power battery is located in the area traditionally housing the gasoline tank. The power controller is also below the hood. Power flow is then to the electric motor which is equipped

---

*One British Thermal Unit (Btu) is the quantity of heat required to raise one pound of water one degree Fahrenheit at its point of maximum density. The heat of combustion of one gallon of gasoline yields 127,600 Btu. One kilowatt-hour (kwh) equals 3,413 Btu. If the vehicle uses 0.3 kwh per mile average in residential and metropolitan (urban) driving, it requires 1,030 Btu per mile. 127,600/1,030 = 123 mi/gal.

with feet that sit on the original engine mounting. The shaft of the motor connects into the standard manual transmission, and the power is transferred to the wheels by means of the differential.

Top speed of this vehicle for both models is close to 60 mph. Acceleration is 0-30 mph in eight seconds. Urban driving range on a single charge is 35 miles. In a ten-hour day, with charging while the vehicle is parked, the daily driving range would be about 60 miles. Such a vehicle as the Thunderbolt, as a high-production vehicle, has many options. In the Thunderbolt, the auxiliary 12-volt battery for lights, horn, windshield wiper, etc., is charged by an alternator with a belt-driven power pick-off from the electric motor shaft.

PERSONAL VAN CLASS ELECTRIC VEHICLES

The LinearVan shown in Figure 8 is another high-performance vehicle. With a curb weight of 5500 pounds, the vehicle has a top speed of 60 mph, an acceleration of 0-30 mph in ten seconds, and a useful range in urban driving of 25-30 miles. In all except range, the vehicle can be equivalent to its gasoline-consuming competition. The 230-volt on-board charger is mounted under the front hood, providing charging current to a rear-mounted battery pod. The power controller and the electric motor are located under the front hood, as in the GameTime 120 and the Woody 120. Likewise, the motor, mounted on the original engine blocks, connects directly to the transmission. An alternator belt-powered pick-off serves to charge the auxiliary 12-volt battery.

Electric vans of this type have been delivered to customers from the smallest size commercially available to those carrying 13 passengers and driver. Again, because these vans are high-production vehicles, many options are available.

Electric-powered vans are best suited for regular prescribed runs. Airports, marinas, hospital grounds, military bases, dock areas, large manufacturing grounds and campuses are examples of areas where this vehicle will prove useful.

ELECTRIC VEHICLES FOR PARAPLEGICS*

When speaking with personnel in a rehabilitation center, one soon learns that public transportation, faced everywhere with financial difficulties, fails to serve the needs of the handicapped. Moreover, the cost of private transportation to move a wheelchair occupant from home to hospital to home can be a day's pay or more. What is the solution?

---

*The word is used here to include all who might benefit from such a specialized vehicle.

Figure 8. Under the hood, the "LinearVan" propulsion system bears little resemblance to the original Dodge engine. But the van's exterior remains virtually unchanged— except for the "Electric Van" inscription added by its new owner, a Wisconsin electric utility. Top speed is 60 mph. Acceleration is 0-30 mph in eight sec. Single-charge range in urban driving is 25-30 miles. Ten-hour range: 70 miles. Courtesy: Electrical Apparatus.

A vehicle the patient himself can drive may offer the most pragmatic answer. Such a vehicle, designed especially for the handicapped, must meet a wide range of patient needs, all different and individual. The development of the modern high-performance electric vehicle and the advent of miniature solid-state controls has revealed new vistas of personal travel for paraplegics at speeds comparable to those of gasoline powered cars.

With an estimated 40,000 Americans losing self-locomotion annually from accidents and disease, adding to the more than one million already afflicted, the breakthrough represented by the high-performance electric vehicle has come none too soon. Thousands of these handicapped people previously enjoyed automobile driving and yearn again for the freedom of the road with a vehicle under personal command. Thus equipped, the paraplegic can achieve a renewed feeling of independence.

A vehicle designed for a paraplegic is one the operator can independently enter in a wheelchair, whether hand-propelled or electric. It must be a vehicle the operator can command from his chair. To achieve these results, the floor of the vehicle should be flat and at minimum height above the pavement. Then on approach, the person in a wheelchair can cause a code signal to be emitted that unlocks and opens the door, after which a small gangplank is lowered enabling the wheelchair and its occupant to enter the vehicle. The chair may then be locked into position and becomes the driver's seat.

On either side of the central section of the car, and to the rear of the driver, are seats under which are located the motive power batteries. These sources of energy are in a rectangular tube on either side of the vehicle. For infrequently required servicing, the batteries, riding an internal pallet, may be withdrawn from the rear of the vehicle. Where the steering wheel is found in conventional vehicles, a small panel is located, serving as the control console of the vehicle. A button on this panel closes and locks the entrance door.

To drive the vehicle, the driver depresses the magnetic interlock button. This starts current flow from the battery to the controller, and in turn to the motor. A small lever with motion forward and backward serves to select the direction of motion and the rate of acceleration. This lever, returned to the neutral position and pressed sideways provides braking action. Locked in this position, it serves as the emergency brake.

A second small lever, which may be operated with the same hand that controls the first lever, with sidewise motion gives guidance to the vehicle. Thus, using the levers on the control console, the driver has complete command of vehicle doors, movement, acceleration, steering, braking, lighting and signaling.

Electric vehicles have an inherent advantage for paraplegics which conventional powered cars lack. The electric vehicle has greater flexibility in structure and controls allowing customized features vital to paraplegics. The low floor, permitting wheelchair mounting with a small inclined plane, affords a safety factor absent in lift operations. There is adequate electric energy for the full range of commands given by the driver in both routine use and road emergencies. Since the electric car is a non-emission vehicle, the paraplegic can safely drive it inside buildings. Because electric vehicles have a high record of reliability, the paraplegic, who can drive only the car fitted for him, is seldom inconvenienced. The chassis of fabricated aluminum, the body of fiberglass, the almost indestructible electric modules, give the paraplegic an endurable, highly dependable means of personal transportation.

Such a high-performance vehicle, with batteries electrically charged with an on-board charger from an outlet either at home or work, now allows 100 miles of urban driving in a ten-hour day. Such vehicles can be made available thanks to recent developments in solid state controls miniaturization, and the maturing of electric vehicle design. Clearly, the use of specially designed electric vehicles will assure paraplegics similar freedom of movement, now largely denied to them, but traditionally accorded other segments of the population.

GOVERNMENT REGULATIONS AND SPECIFICATIONS

A serious danger to the well-being, future prosperity, and rapid progress of the electric vehicle industry for the benefit of the public it serves is the possibility of adverse action by the federal government in the guise of a well-meaning act. The imposition of design specifications is unwise if done in excessive detail.

For greatest benefit to the citizenry, electric vehicle manufacturers should have the widest possible latitude in design during this formative and innovative period. The 1966 National Traffic and Motor Vehicle Safety Act and amendments serve to protect the public. Now the industry, while minuscule, is in transition. Departure from Detroit conversions is not only imminent but going forward. The public will soon be introduced to electric vehicles which have been designed from the ground up as electric cars.

This change provides chassis of rust-proof material impervious even to road salt in the snow latitudes. Bodies will be of fiberglass or similar materials as illustrated in Figure 1. These vehicle components have the long life to match the almost fault-free service that has been established with the electric modules, including the battery charger, the power controller and the motor. The batteries should be considered the vehicle's fuel supply, consumed over the years.

If, by governmental regulation, the nation fails to permit innovations, America will assume a second position in this field behind Japan, England and Germany. Each of these nations currently is advancing rapidly.

The danger of federal specifications in design, other than safety specifications, is already being seen in action through the General Service Administration's attempt to standardize electric trucks procured by the government. It is much too early for such minute specifications, if indeed they are ever desirable. The electric vehicle industry, unlike the internal combustion vehicle industry, is in the process of formation. Changes are rapidly appearring that tend to make yesterday's positions obsolete. Thus, specifications are now being issued that call for steel bodies, while current indications are that fiberglass bodies may be preferable. The quantities of electric vehicles now absorbable by the market are particularly adaptable to fiberglass construction. The utility industry, for instance, is employing fiberglass rather than steel in IC truck bodies for some uses. The British, with continuous production of electric trucks underway, are now heavily committed to plastic bodies.

Freedom from excessively detailed specifications at this time will assure better vehicles for the government, and more importantly for the people who ultimately pay for the vehicles concerned. Innovative concepts not yet conceived will be possible. They will be brought forth by both domestic and foreign manufacturers. The concept of competition will be strengthened, which by the very nature of any proposed specifications is severely limited. Long-lasting electric vehicles are possible. One's second car can be like his home. Innovative design can mean that only one or two second cars are needed over a lifetime. The British have examples of electric trucks operating 20, 30 and even more years.

The best way to indicate how regulation and specification have damaged an emerging industry may be to cite history. Consider the field of transportation in England, the country where Adam Smith, the original apostle of free enterprise lived, and America, where free enterprise came to its greatest fulfillment.

In America, the first electric vehicle was assembled by Fred M. Kimball of Boston in 1888.[7] If the design of electric vehicles had been fixed by edict, in seven years the horseless carriage of 1895 (Figure 9) would have resulted. Notice that the thinking of the designers at that time carried the mental baggage of the past. The vehicle used was converted from a Victoria. Only the horse is absent. Such thinking is natural. Thought processes generally are evolutionary. With our present knowledge of what was then the future, we know that the general concept of the automobile in its present form only began to take shape in about 1902. Vehicular design at the turn of the century was dynamic. The early pattern can be seen today in that the modern revival of high-performance electric vehicles is only eight years old, and only now are we witnessing departures of electric vehicles from the familiar Detroit products. To the everlasting credit of the transportation

Figure 9. The electric Victoria had a curb weight of 2400 pounds of which 900 pounds were batteries, yielding a ratio of 37%. The two 2½ hp motors gave a maximum speed of 12 mph, and with four passengers was stated to have a range of 30 miles. On hard, level roads the average current consumption was 26 amperes. The two motors drove the rear wheels independently of one another. The vehicle had four gradations of speed (battery voltage switching) of 5, 7½, 10 and 12 mph. All wheels had ball-bearing axles, the rear wheels having a diameter of 40 inches, with front wheels of 34 inches in diameter. Courtesy Northwestern University.

group in the newly constituted Energy Research and Development Agency (ERDA), encouragement is being given to a fresh approach in the creation of electric vehicles. Eventually from this funding and independent effort, concepts in electric vehicles highly advantageous to the public will appear.

While there was no effort by the U.S. government to issue specifications on early vehicles emerging from American shops and barns in the 19th and early 20th centuries, Britain in 1865 legislated on mechanical road vehicles,[8] restricting the speed of steam trucks (shown in Figure 10) to 4 mph in open country, and to 2 mph in the city (though the trucks were capable of 20 mph). Legislation also required that each vehicle be preceded by a man carrying a red flag.

It was not until 1878 that an amendment banished the flag, but not the man. It was not until 1896 that the man was eliminated and the speed limit

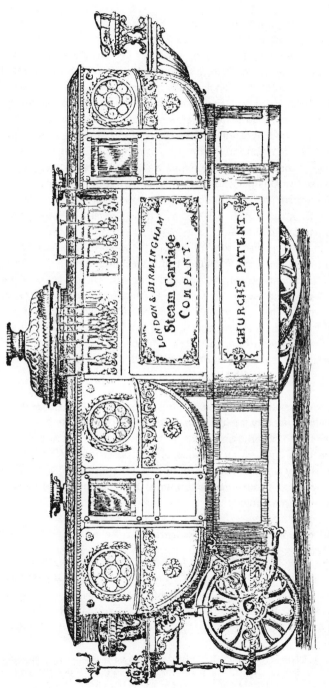

Figure 10. Dr. William Church's steam carriage of 1832. Walter Hancock at about the same time constructed an assortment of nine steam carriages, all of which operated. One of his routes, inaugurated between Paddington and London, had a road distance of about four miles. Oliver and Berkebile reported "One of his better vehicles weighed about 7000 pounds and carried 16 passengers. Two vertical cylinders, nine inches in diameter and with a 12-inch stroke, drove a crank shaft connected by a chain to driving wheels 48 inches in diameter. Steam was supplied by a sheet-flue boiler, two feet square and three feet high, that was situated over a grate having a closed ashpit and a fair draft." Courtesy Smithsonian Press.

raised. But the damage had been done. Excessive regulation had killed mechanical over-the-road transportation in England. The palm of development thus passed to the Continent. And while the Crown's bureaucracy was stifling English initiative, N. A. Otto, a German physician, in 1867 invented a four-cycle internal combustion engine that ran on illuminating gas. Taking this concept, in 1885, Gottlieb Daimler, another German, devised an engine of the same type fueled by gasoline. That same year Carl Benz drove a three-wheeled vehicle propelled by the Daimler engine. Benz went to France and leased the rights of his invention to the Panhard-Levassor company. Thus began the French automobile industry, while England was shackled by legislation. Both Benz and Daimler came to America. In 1888 each applied for and received American patents, though an American, George B. Selden of Rochester, New York, on May 8, 1879, applied for a patent on what today is recognized as an automobile.[9]

Continuing innovative leadership in Europe, Rudolph Diesel* in 1892 patented the internal combustion engine which bears his name. Yet while Continental developments came rapidly and England suffered under repressive legislation, the genius of the practical American inventor came to the forefront. America gave mechanical wheels to the average person, and in so doing, transformed personal transportation. First America and then all the advanced nations of the world were affected. This progress was accomplished without governmental regulation during the fledgling years of the industry. The analogy is relevant for the fledgling electric vehicle industry at the present time.

The author, with possible redundancy, thus repeats: A serious danger to the electric vehicle industry as it emerges Phoenix-like from its cocoon is the aggressiveness of a government, however well-meaning, in attempting to regulate and specify. The destiny of personal transportation in America will not be determined by detailed specifications carefully contrived. New concepts, now almost beyond our imagination, must be freely evolved to assure optimum progress for mankind.

Standards for Electric Vehicle Charging Receptacles

To the driver of electric vehicles, one of the most important considerations is the ready availability of electrical outlets suitable for charging the battery. Is there an outlet? Will the charging cord plug fit the receptacle available? Affirmative answers to these questions are essential. To increase the ease of driving and to encourage the use of electric vehicles, standards for electrical

---

*Rudolph Diesel (1858-1913) was born in Paris of German parents and educated at the Munich Polytechnic School. In 1893 he published *The Theory and Construction of a Rational Heat Motor.* He was drowned as a result of falling from a ferry boat.

receptacles must be established. During these early stages of electric vehicular development, such considerations should be actively promoted.

The electric service available at an outlet is basically established by the utility electric supply furnished to the structure containing the outlet. The existing wiring in the structure is also important. Finally, the electric code of the community is a relevant factor. Aboard the vehicle, the rate at which the battery will accept current and the battery voltage are important. Fortunately, the limitation is not in the battery. The current acceptance rate of a vehicle battery exceeds many electrical distribution networks. Considering the above, in the Chicago area, and with cooperation from the local utility, there has been a standard established for both the Consumer's Electric Vehicle and the Commercial (heavy) Electric Vehicle.

For the Consumer's Electric Vehicle, the electric outlet is a "receptacle 15-amp, 125-volt, two-pole, three-wire, grounding type receptacle with attachment plug."[10] This outlet is shown in Figure 11.

Figure 11. Consumer's Electric Vehicle receptacle. 125-volt, 15-ampere, 2-pole, 3-wire, grounding type, with attachment plug.

For the Commercial (heavy) Electric Vehicle, the electric outlet is a "250-volt, 2-pole, 3-wire, grounding type receptacle and attachment plug."[10] This outlet is shown in Figure 12.

Figure 12. Commercial (Heavy) Electric Vehicle receptacle. 250-volts, 2-pole, 3-wire, grounding type, with attachment plug.

In setting forth these standards, one must consider not only conditions now, but must also judge future vehicle needs as well. While an electric vehicle conversion such as that of the Thunderbolt 240 currently carries about 18 kwh of energy, the gasoline version with a 12-gallon tank contains an energy equivalent of about 450 kwh.

In urban driving, the Thunderbolt achieves an energy equivalence of 65 miles per gallon, while a subcompact achieves about one-third that figure. So the 450 kwh shrinks to 150 kwh because of the differences in drive system efficiencies. It is apparent, therefore, as batteries with greater energy density are developed, more kwh will be placed aboard the electric vehicle to enhance range. To have a reasonable charging time, the rate of charge becomes important.

The rate at which energy is requested from a distribution system in electric terminology is known as demand. If, for example, the energy to be placed aboard future vehicles is 30 kwh, there should be provision for filling batteries in, let us say, ten hours. The efficiency of a charger is about 75%. To place 30 kwh in the batteries requires 30/0.75 = 40 kwh to be purchased. In ten hours that is a 4-kw demand. A 4-kw demand at 120 volts would require 4000/120 = 33 amperes. In practice, this would more likely approximate 40 amperes, because power factor* here becomes important. For 4-kw demand at 230 volts, 25 amperes is required. The only electric supply permitted by the electrical code would be 230 volts at 30 amperes. To be generous when viewing the future, 230-volt, 50-ampere receptacles should be provided for high-performance electric vehicles.

While driving electric vehicles extensively in the Chicago, Illinois; Madison, Wisconsin; and Springfield, Illinois areas, we have learned that the only common electric receptacles externally available are rated at 120 volts. This is probably true for most of America. An on-board 120-volt charger will enable the vehicle owner to obtain a booster charge with relative ease at service stations, motels and automobile dealer agencies.

For every hour an electric vehicle is charged from such an outlet, it will be able to travel 2-4 miles or more, due to depolarization of the battery. Basic charging probably will occur at night, a schedule which would also better serve the nation's generating equipment and distribution facilities.

Accessible electric receptacles for 240 volts commonly** have been found only in automobile repair shops equipped to perform electric welding. Often

---

*A charger is both a resistive and reactive load. A higher charging current for such a load is required for a given kw than if the load were purely resistive.

**The author has collected many amusing experiences in the course of requesting a 240-volt receptacle for an electric vehicle. It is like automobiling in the 1910s or yachting before World War I. In 1976, an electric vehicle is still so unique, the driver is seldom refused even though his request might require special effort from those contacted for assistance.

an outlet has not been readily available. Such outlets, which could be considered part of the essential infrastructure for electric vehicles, will become available only as electric vehicles become more common.

Recognizing the existing situation, it is recommended that high-performance electric vehicles carry on-board a 120-volt charger, and have at the home base a battery charger capable of using a 240-volt, 50-ampere receptacle.

The author recognizes that for many, the 120-volt on-board charger will adequately satisfy the need for electric energy. As Table I indicates, 87% of the trips made by Americans cover 15 miles or less. A 15-mile trip requires 5-8 kwh in a high-performance electric vehicle. A 120-volt, 10-ampere on-board charger can, with a demand of 1 kw, replenish the battery in 5-8 hours.

POWER AND ENERGY REQUIREMENTS

To move an electric vehicle at highway speeds requires substantial power. There is the initial power demanded for acceleration. Then immediately there is the power needed to overcome rolling resistance. And finally, as speed is gained, the opposition due to windage must be offset. These power needs are in addition to the losses in the drive train itself. Fortunately, the efficiency of the electric power train is four to five times greater than the drive train of the internal combustion vehicle, as will later be shown.

Power and Energy for Driving Needs

The power required for a 6000-pound van with a frontal area of 36 square feet has been conveniently plotted by Dr. Gordon J. Murphy[11] in Figures 13A, 13B and 13C. Referring to Figure 13A, notice that at the national speed limit of 55 mph, about 50 hp is required for cruising. The cruising curve is observed to rise more rapidly as the speed increases. This type curve is known as one having an exponential slope. This ever-steepening feature is due to an ever-greater share of the power required to overcome windage. Every driver has learned how much less gasoline is needed to travel between two cities if the 55 mph speed limit is obeyed rather than the earlier 70-80 mph speeds. The same reasoning applies to electric vehicles. In this figure, the peak power during acceleration rises initially because of the choice made by Dr. Murphy in his selection of acceleration made at each speed, plus the effect of windage.

Apparent from the three curves is that substantial power is required to obtain a high-performance vehicle. Inasmuch as 1.33 horsepower, when units are converted, becomes one kilowatt, a term found more useful in discussing power characteristics of electric vehicles, the numbers on the vertical scale of

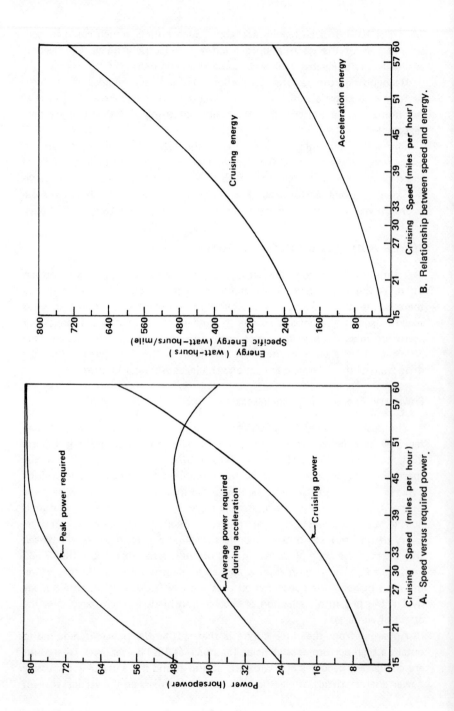

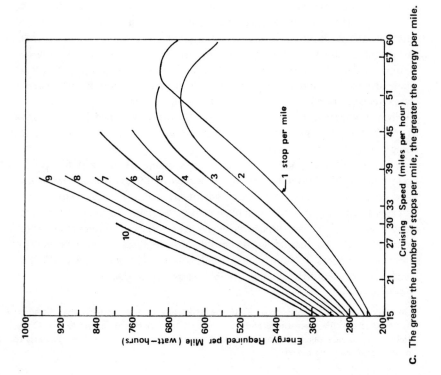

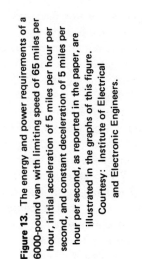

Figure 13. The energy and power requirements of a 6000-pound van with limiting speed of 65 miles per hour, initial acceleration of 5 miles per hour per second, and constant deceleration of 5 miles per hour per second, as reported in the paper, are illustrated in the graphs of this figure.
Courtesy: Institute of Electrical and Electronic Engineers.

C. The greater the number of stops per mile, the greater the energy per mile.

this graph can also be read, as a rule of thumb,* as kilowatts which must be delivered from the battery to sustain this performance. A battery to store one kilowatt-hour of energy weighs about 65 pounds. A van carrying 1500 pounds of batteries at the 55 mph speed, would discharge them in about 24 minutes. During this period, the vehicle would have traveled approximately 22 miles.

In practice, the van while initially traveling at 55 mph, would, as more and more energy was taken from the battery, gradually go slower, particularly after 12-15 miles. On the other hand, if the speed limit in urban areas were 30 mph, the van's batteries would need to provide power at the rate of only 12 kw rather than 50 kw. Then the van's range would be 30-40 miles. The energy required per mile would be less, not only because of reduced windage, but because a battery can provide more deliverable energy if it can be used at a lower discharge rate. This exercise has been useful, however, to indicate that electric vehicles are for urban application and ideally at slower speeds.

Let us now determine the energy required per mile when the number of stops per mile varies. Such driving conditions are more typical of city driving. Figure 13B is a plot showing cruising speed in miles per hour versus energy required per mile driven. As in the former case, the limiting factor is the deliverable energy contained in the battery. Figure 13C indicates that whatever the cruising speed may be, the greater number of stops per mile, the greater is the requirement of energy per mile. For this reason, the discerning reader of electric vehicle advertising literature must always question what is meant by the *range of the vehicle* unless the manufacturer clearly states the conditions of driving used to determine the range.

From the graphs it can be seen that at a cruising speed of 30 mph, twice as much energy is required to travel one mile with 10 stops per mile, as compared to 1 stop per mile.

While the above graphs were based on a computer study with a 6000-pound van, a 2000-pound curb weight vehicle with less frontal area would yield consistently lower power requirements as well as energy needs. But in all cases substantial power and energy must be available for high-performance electric vehicles. When discussing power and energy requirements of these vehicles, it can be instructive to consider the relatively high efficiency of electrical elements: Controllers, 95-97%; power transformers, 93-98%, electric motors, 80-90%; charger, 75-85%; battery, 70-80%.

---

*One kilowatt = 1.33 horsepower. If the efficiency of the electric drive system is assumed to be 75%, then the battery to supply 1 kw must provide 1/0.75 = 1.33 kw. Hence, in the case taken, the numbers on the vertical can also be read as kilowatts to be delivered from the battery.

Often one is involved in discussion of efficiency comparisons between electric cars and gasoline-powered cars. One of the best studies on this subject has been done by Salihi,[1 2] from whom the figures below were obtained.

The average efficiency of the electric car is defined as the ratio of road energy per mile to the a-c energy supplied to the battery charger. Over the Federal Driving Cycle for a 3150-pound, conventional-shaped car, it is 32.4%, by calculation. The average system efficiency is defined as the ratio of road energy per mile to the supplied heat energy in coal or other fuel consumed by the electric-generating plant. For the same car it is 10.3% as shown in Table II.

Table II. Efficiency and Energy Requirements over the Federal Driving Cycle for a 3150-lb Reference Electric Car of Body Design and Road Losses Similar to a Conventional Heat Engine Car of Equal Weight

Heat energy in fuel fed into the power-generating plant	2.23 kwh/mi
	7620 Btu/mi
AC energy fed into the battery charger	0.71 kwh/mi
Energy delivered by the battery during discharge comprising of:	
road energy—0.34 kwh/mi; accessories—0.17 kwh/mi	0.51 kwh/mi
Road energy at wheels	0.23 kwh/mi
Efficiency of electric car (road energy/energy fed to charger)	32.4%
Overall system efficiency (road energy/heat energy in fuel fed into the generating plant)	10.3%

The drive system efficiency of a gasoline-powered car is about 15%. The average efficiency of this car is defined as the ratio of road energy per mile to the heat energy in the gasoline contained in the fuel tank. It is given as 8.3%. The average system efficiency is defined as the ratio of road energy per mile to the associated heat energy in crude oil fed into the refinery. It is given as 7.1%.

Thus, the electric car and the gasoline car, in terms of fuel from the ground, have comparable efficiencies of 10.3% and 7.1% respectively. The overall energy requirement for the electric vehicle is about 72% of the requirement for the gasoline-powered car. As proponents of electric cars are quick to point out, electric energy is a versatile power source obtained from coal, petroleum, nuclear energy, water power, and in the future possibly from geothermal, solar, wind and tidal power.

Discussing the efficiencies above (apparent from Tables II and III), reference is made to the Federal Driving Cycle (FDC). The FDC is a prescribed driving cycle of accelerations, constant speeds, decelerations, and stops over

Table III. Efficiency and Energy Requirements for a 3150-lb Baseline Conventional Heat Engine Car Over the Federal Driving Cycle

Heat energy in crude oil fed into the refinery	3.26 kwh/mi
	11,100 Btu/mi
Heat energy consumed in gasoline of fuel tank	2.77 kwh/mi
	9,450 Btu/mi
Road energy at wheels	0.23 kwh/mi
Average efficiency of heat engine car (road energy/energy consumed in gasoline)	8.3%
Overall average system efficiency (road energy/heat energy in crude oil)	7.1%

a given length of time. Its purpose is to make comparisons on an equal basis in various sections of the country. Such a test is shown in Figure 14. The cycle covers a total driving distance of 7.5 miles over a total period of 1370 seconds. The average speed during this cycle is 19.6 mph. Tables IV and V are respectively[13] *Test Schedule for Residential Driving Cycle* and *Test Schedule for Metropolitan Area Driving Cycle.*

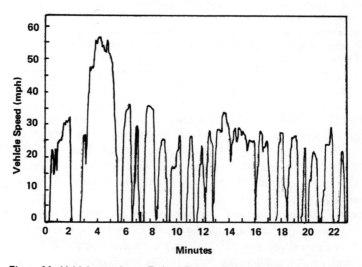

Figure 14. Vehicle speed over Federal Driving Cycle. Courtesy: Institute of Electrical and Electronic Engineers.

Both heating and air-conditioning were included in the above calculations for the electric and the gasoline-powered car. These subjects, together with power-steering if used, are discussed in the overall design of the electric car.

Table IV. Test Schedule for Residential Driving Cycle [a]

Mode	Average Acceleration (mph/sec)	Time (sec)	Cumulative Time (sec)
Idle	0	20	20
0-30 mph	2.14	14	34
30 mph constant	0	15	49
30-15 mph	-1.37	11	60
15 mph constant	0	15	75
15-30 mph	1.20	12.5	87.5
30 mph constant	0	46.5	134
30-20 mph	-1.20	8	142
20-0 mph	-2.50	8	150
Repeat cycle			

[a]The end point of driving range is defined as the point at which the vehicle has ceased to meet the prescribed driving schedule in terms of acceleration or maximum speed.

Table V. Test Schedule for Metropolitan Area Driving Cycle

Mode	Average Acceleration (mph/sec)	Time (sec)	Cumulative Time (sec)
Idle	0	20	20
0-30 mph	2.14	14	34
30 mph constant	0	15	49
30-15	-1.37	11	60
15 mph constant	0	15	75
15-45 mph	1.20	25	100
45 mph constant	0	21	121
40-20 mph	-1.19	21	142
20-0 mph	-2.50	8	150

Since these amenities of transportation are energy users, consuming 33% of the total energy in the calculations above, they should be considered in this section.

Heating, Air Conditioning and Power Steering*

In the motive power battery of a high-performance consumer's electric vehicle, one may place 12 kilowatt-hours of available energy. In filling the gas tank of a subcompact car, 450 equivalent kilowatt-hours of energy are placed aboard. If the electric drive system is considered more efficient than the IC drive system by a factor of four, the gasoline-powered vehicle still has ten times more energy at its driver's disposal than does the electric car. For accessory power-use, the former has 40-50 times more energy available. Inevitably, the electric vehicle owner begins to think conservatively about energy. He avoids jack rabbit starts. He looks ahead at the traffic light and coasts if the light is red. In general, he refrains from pushing his car quite so hard. As a result, many thoughtful persons believe that the useful life of an electric car will easily be twice that of a conventional IC car.

Heating

In the northern latitudes of the United States, in Canada, Europe, and Japan, as well as other temperate latitude locations, heating will be essential for electric vehicles. In more southern latitudes, a heater may be optional equipment.

Two sources of energy are available for electric car heating to assure bodily comfort. One is a petroleum-base source of power. The other is electric energy.

In larger electric vehicles (Figure 8), gasoline heaters have been used successfully. And gasoline is everywhere present. Propane heaters may be employed, but source supplies are less abundant. The second source for heat is to use the energy stored in the electric battery. In a high-performance consumer electric vehicle, well sealed, a 1000-watt blower heater can yield body comfort. During urban driving, such a heater would utilize 10-15% of the power that would otherwise be available for driving. Range, consequently, might be reduced by the same percentage.

Alternatively, a smaller blower may be used for warming the feet, supplemented by an electrically heated seat. The latter, being contact warming, is a far more efficient means of providing acceptable body comfort. It is analagous to the heating pad in bed. The heat available from the motor, for most driving, is negligible and may be disregarded.

---

*The author and his associates fulfilled a contract to investigate heating and cooling from the more exotic batteries of the future. From the molten salt class of battery, more heat than is required will be available for heating. But the heat absorption principle applied to air-conditioning offers little hope currently, because of the resulting size and weight of the equipment required.

This conclusion may be seen from calculation. Suppose the vehicle requires an average power of 8 kilowatts in urban driving. Suppose that the integrated efficiency of the motor is 70%. This means a heat loss of 30% is available, which when multiplied by 8 kilowatts is 2400 watts, equivalent of the heat from a good electric oven. Most of that heat will be trapped in the heat-sink capacity of the iron and copper of the motor, and will gradually radiate into the surrounding air. It is not immediately available.

Air Conditioning

When the sun's rays are vertical, almost one kilowatt-hour is received each hour on the earth's surface, or on the horizontal surface of an automobile for each square yard exposed. What about air conditioning an electric car? This can be done, but the range of the vehicle will be reduced approximately 15%* if cooling is accomplished in the conventional manner. The question that must then be asked is: Do you use the electric vehicle as you would your gasoline-powered car?

The answer is that you can't, because there is insufficient range. Thus, the electric car will be occupied for periods, on the average, much shorter than those in the IC vehicle. The electrical vehicle will be utilized for trips lasting 5-30 minutes.

With these facts in mind, the question of air conditioning an electric vehicle can be approached in three ways: Provide conventional air conditioning using a belt power-pick off, use a battery-powered dc motor running the air conditioner, or place an ac motor aboard the car to run the air conditioner while the vehicle is charging.

In the latter case, one enters a "cold" vehicle. On disconnecting the power cord from the receptacle, the car will warm gradually; but even in the hottest climate, if the windows are closed, the car will be comfortable. On arriving at the destination, the air conditioner again will need to be plugged in, and the charter also connected.

Of the three methods, the first is least expensive but reduces effective range. The third method is less expensive than the second, but adds weight to the vehicle. Most expensive is the second method, installing an auxiliary dc motor on-board to operate the air conditioner.

Power Steering

An electrical vehicle can be equipped with power steering. Modern high-performance consumer's electric vehicles have curb weights equal to or exceeding by a small amount that of a subcompact car. While the versatility

---

*Salihi[12] uses 3 hp.

of electric energy and the ingenuity of engineers permit almost any inanimate physical task to be performed by electricity, a central question should be asked: Are the added complexity and expense desirable in order to power steer a small, lightweight, second or third family car in the daily transportation routine? Power steering would reduce the vehicle's range probably less than 5%, making the choice essentially one of economy.

THE ECONOMICS OF ELECTRIC VEHICLES

What are the economic factors concerning electric vehicles? Figure 15 has been developed[14] to help determine electric vehicle breakeven cost sensitivity to annual miles traveled.

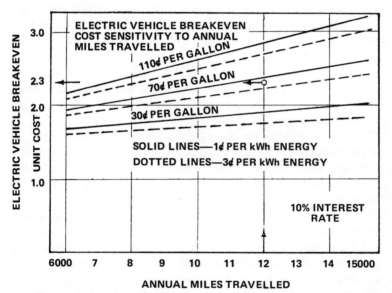

Figure 15. Electric vehicle breakeven cost sensitivity to annual miles traveled.

In simpler words, how much can I afford to pay for an electric vehicle? For the case illustrated in Figure 15, consider travel to be 12,000 miles per year. Assume gasoline costs to be 70¢ per gallon and incremental electric rates are 2¢ per kwh. Reading the graph, you could afford to pay 2.3 times what the equivalent gasoline-powered vehicle would cost. If the comparable car would be a subcompact at $4000, you could pay 2.3 x $4000 = $9200 for an electric car.

Consider the second case, in which the electric vehicle is the second or even the third car in a family unit. Assume 6000 miles per year, 70¢ gasoline, and 3¢ per kwh. In this case, you could afford to pay 1.9 x $4000 = $7600 for an electric car in 1976 dollars.

Following is a carefully developed family of curves based on the relative life of internal combustion cars and electric cars, the miles per gallon for the former, their relative maintenance cost,* and interest rates.

When all factors are weighed, in broad terms one can afford to pay a surprisingly higher first cost for an electric vehicle than for an IC car. The reasons will become clear as these pages are studied. William H. Shafer, of the Chicago-based Commonwealth Edison Company, calculated in an independent study** that the Woody 120 bearing a sales price 1.76 times greater than the sales price of a subcompact has the same cost per mile of life. But then, the reader will agree there are many factors in the marketing of electric vehicles independent of cost. Still a cost analysis does yield an objective means of measurement.

The validity of Figure 15 is further substantiated in a study by P. A. Nelson et al.[15] Nelson's report includes the graph presented in Figure 16. In this graph, the cost of gasoline and electric energy appear on the horizontal, while fuel cost per mile is presented on the vertical. Constructing the graph, the automobile load weight was considered to be 2800 pounds, energy required at the wheel 0.22 kwh per ton-mile, an urban driving profile, and reasonably assumed efficiencies for both electric and gasoline-powered automobiles.

To read Figure 16, assume gasoline is 75¢ per gallon and incremental electric energy cost is 3¢ per kwh. Rising vertically to the average of the two lines representing electric vehicles, fuel cost is about 1½¢ per mile. Using gasoline, it is nearly 4¢ per mile. However, if the amortized battery cost is also taken into account as fuel cost, then the fuel costs are more nearly equal.

Finally, what impact will the use of electricity have on the electric utility industry in America? Tiny. That clearly seems the answer. The impact will be slight, as Table VI (by P. A. Nelson et al.[16]) indicates. In this table, the columns, left to right, are years, total electric vehicles in use, total production of electric energy in kwh per year, kwh required for battery recharge based on electric cars driving 10,000 miles per year, 0.5 kwh of electric energy used per mile by the electric car, and a battery charging efficiency of 70%.

---

*In Britain, with about 60,000 electric trucks in use, it has been reported that an electric vehicle has between one-fourth and one-third the maintenance cost of an equivalent IC vehicle.

**Private communication based on relative gasoline and electric energy costs in 1976.

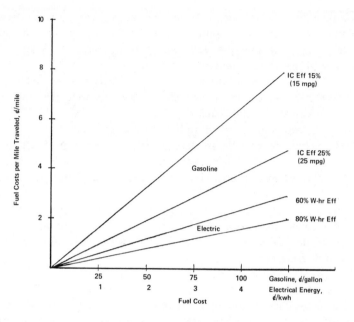

Figure 16. Fuel costs per mile of operation for electric and gasoline-powered automobiles.

Table VI. Electrical Energy Required to Recharge Electric Vehicles

| Year | No. of Electric Cars | Electrical Energy, kwh/yr | | |
		Total U.S. Production	Required for Battery Recharge	Percent of Total Used by Electric Cars
1985	2×10^5	4.3×10^{12}	1.0×10^9	0.02
2000	1.8×10^7	1.0×10^{13}	9×10^{10}	0.9

In the last column, Dr. Nelson indicates 0.02% of the electric energy would be consumed by electric vehicles, rising to only 0.9% in the year 2000. One concludes that the effect of electric vehicles on America's electric generating capacity would be minimal.

Before discussing the elements of electric vehicles in detail, it would be useful to review terminology and the basics of electricity. To understand what happens electrically in the drive train as the accelerator is pushed, the reader is invited to obtain broader knowledge of electricity, the vehicle's battery charger, the batteries, the circuit-breaker, the controller and finally the electric motor. All are considered on the following pages.

REFERENCES

1. U.S. Department of Transportation/Federal Highway Administration. Nationwide Personal Transportation Study, Report 10—Purposes of Automotive Trips and Travel (1975).
2. Motor Vehicle Manufacturers Association of the United States. *1973/ 1974 Automotive Facts & Figures.* Detroit, Michigan (1974).
3. Hamilton, W. F. "Impact of Future Use of Electric Cars in the Los Angeles Region," U.S. Environmental Protection Agency, Ann Arbor, Michigan (1974).
4. Schwartz, H. J. "The Computer Simulation of Automobile Use Patterns for Defining Battery Requirements for Electric Cars," NASA TM X-71900 Lewis Research Center, Cleveland, Ohio 44135.
5. Thoreau, Henry David. *Walden* (New York: Crown Publishers, 1970).
6. Federal Energy Administration. "Tips for Energy Savers," Conservation and Environment, U.S. Government Printing Office, 0-566-806 (1975).
7. Whitney, Albert W. "Man and the Motorcar," State of Illinois (1938), p. 267.
8. Oliver, S. H. and D. A. Berkebile. *The Smithsonian Collection of Automobiles and Motorcycles* (Washington, D.C.: Smithsonian Press, 1968), p. 164.
9. Partridge, Bellamy. *Fill 'er Up* (New York: McGraw-Hill Book Co., 1952), p. 235.
10. American National Standards C73.13 (1972).
11. Murphy, Gordon J. "Considerations in the Design of Drive Systems for On-the-Road Electric Vehicles," *Proc. IEEE* (December 1972), pp. 1519-1533.
12. Salihi, Jalal T. "Energy Requirements for Electric Cars and Their Impact on Electric Power Generation and Distribution," *IEEE Transactions on Industry Applications,* Vol. 1A-9, No. 5 (1973).
13. Society of Automotive Engineers, Inc. *Federal Driving Cycle,* 1975 SAE Handbook, Warrendale, Pennsylvania, p. 1074.
14. Wakefield, Ernest H. "The Economics of Electric Vehicles in a Fuel Short Nation," Third International Electric Vehicle Symposium, Washington, D.C. (February 19, 1974).
15. Nelson, P. A., A. A. Chelenskas and R. K. Steuneberg. "The Need for Development of High-Energy Batteries for Electric Automobiles," Argonne National Laboratory, ANL-8075 (January 1974).
16. Nelson, P. A. *et al.* ANL High-Energy Batteries for Electric Vehicles," Third International Electric Vehicle Symposium (February 1974).

CHAPTER 2

BASIC ELECTRICITY

"...And when the rain has wet the kite and twine, so that it can conduct the electric fire freely, you will find it stream out plentifully from the key on the approach of your knuckle. At this key the phial may be charged; and from electric fire thus obtained, spirits may be kindled, and all the other electric experiments be performed, which are usually done by the help of a rubbed glass globe or tube, and thereby the sameness of the electric matter with that of lightning completely demonstrated."

Benjamin Franklin to Peter Collinson, 1752

Electricity—carrier of light and power, devourer of time and space, bearer of human speech over land and sea, greatest servant of man, itself unknown.

Charles W. Eliot
Inscription for Union Station
Washington, D.C.

To understand a subject, knowledge of the terminology peculiar to that field is highly desirable. So with electricity. To comprehend accurately, one must have a familiarity with its terms. An expert in a field of study soon recognizes another's proficiency by his word choice. To better understand nature, one must grasp the science of electricity, since all matter consists of atoms, and atoms are bearers of charge. It is through the understanding of these charges, electrons as well as the remaining positive ions, their separation and control, that man has learned to harness vast quantities of energy, providing him with a richer, if not a happier life.

ATOMS AND ELECTRIC CHARGES

Currently 106* different elements have been discovered. Each element has a characteristic atom. The simplest in structure is an atom of hydrogen. This atom consists of a nucleus, where more than 99% of the atom's mass resides, and one orbiting electron. In the nucleus** of the hydrogen atom is one proton bearing a positive charge. The electron carries a negative charge. It is the number of protons in the nucleus which determines the atomic number of an element. The next heaviest atom is helium. Its nucleus has two protons, each bearing a positive charge. Two electrons orbit around this nucleus. The third heaviest atom, containing three protons in its nucleus, is lithium. Lithium bears three orbiting electrons, two circling in an inner orbit, or shell, and one circling alone in an outer shell. The presence of a single electron in an outer shell indicates that such an electron can readily leave the atom and become a free electron. Figure 17 is an illustration of

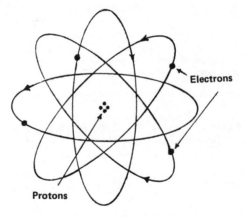

Figure 17. Electrons orbit the nucleus of the atom, and in addition rotate or spin on their own axes. Courtesy Theodore Audel Co.

*Element 106 has not yet (1976) been given a name because of the simultaneity of both the American and Soviet Union experiments by Albert Ghiorso and co-workers at Berkeley California, and G. N. Flerov and colleagues at Dubna, Russia, respectively.
**A nucleus may also contain one or more neutrons. A neutron has no charge but has a mass essentially equal to a proton. The presence of these neutrons serves to increase the mass of the atom, but not its chemical affinity for another element. An atom of lithium, for example, remains lithium even though its nucleus may contain three or four neutrons. Atoms of like atomic number but of different atomic weight are known as isotopes of that element.

four electrons in orbit around a nucleus of four protons, while Figure 18 is successively a symbolic representation of a hydrogen atom of atomic number 1; the helium atom of atomic number 2; the lithium atom of atomic number 3; the oxygen atom of atomic number 8; the fluorine atom of atomic number 9; the neon atom of atomic number 10. These atom representations

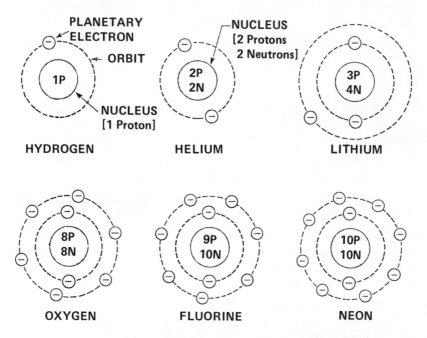

Figure 18. Atomic structure of elements. Courtesy: U.S. Navy Bureau of Personnel.

show helium and neon with their outer shells completely filled. These two are stable atoms and chemically combine with no other atoms. Hydrogen with one electron in its shell will readily bind chemically with an atom whose outer shell lacks but one electron. The same may be said for lithium. Oxygen is short two electrons in its outer shell. When chemically linking, it will be combined with an atom with an outer shell containing two electrons. It is, therefore, the so-called valence electrons which form chemical bonds, joining atoms into molecules. There can be molecules with as few as two atoms, or molecules which are literally skeins of atoms culminating in the life-forming molecules. And always it is the valence electrons providing the bonding. In the newly observed[1] high Rydberg atoms, a hydrogen atom, for example, can be excited so that the radius of the orbiting electron can be made 10,000 times larger than the radius earlier observed. Thus other normal atoms can be found "inside" the high Rydberg atoms, even at very low pressures.

Electrons bear a negative charge. It is the movement of vast numbers of these free electrons in an orderly direction which we recognize as an electric current. For every electron freed, the remaining atom becomes a positive ion. Electrons can move readily in most metals. The separation of atoms into positive ions and free electrons can be useful to man because an electric current is created. Electric charges may be separated or moved in the following ways:

1. By passing a conductor through a magnetic field. Equal quantities of positive and negative charges of electricity appear on opposite ends of the conductor. This principle of a generator is the basis for our electric utility industry.

2. By using the chemistry of batteries. The terminals of a battery are charged with equal and opposite quantities of electricity.

3. By thermionic action. A heated wire allows electrons to escape. These free charges can be attracted to another conductor. This principle is the basis of the television tube and many other related devices.

4. By photovoltaic action. If light waves fall on a conductor, electrons escape and are collected by a separate conductor. The photoelectric cells used in space exploration generate electricity in this manner.

5. By passing radiation through material, atoms are ionized and separated. The operations of ion chambers and Geiger counters are applications of this separation.

6. By polarization. An insulator is brought into a volume of voltage difference, the atoms are distorted and become polarized. An example is the use of mica as the dielectric in a capacitor.

7. By induction. A conductor brought into the neighborhood of already separated electric charges causes free electrons to move on the conductor.

8. By friction between unlike substances. The surface atoms of one material yields electrons to a second material, which then becomes negatively charged. A comb passing through hair is one such example.

9 By pressure applied to certain crystals, such as quartz. If a mechanical force is applied across a quartz crystal a voltage is produced. The interaction between voltage and pressure is known as the piezoelectric effect. This phenomenon is employed in tuned communication circuits.

Electric charges, once separated, establish an electric field. In this electric field there can be conduction of charges, induction, and polarization. By better understanding electric fields, we can better comprehend magnetic fields, because there is an interconnection between electricity and magnetism. The electric charge has its counterpart in unit pole. There are two types of electric charge, positive and negative. Likewise there are two unit poles, north and south. Both the charge and the pole follow similar laws of attraction and repulsion. There are, however, no conductors for magnetic charges as there are for electric charges. Neither can a unit pole be completely isolated, as can an electric charge.

ELECTRIC AND MAGNETIC FIELDS

When a body at one location affects a body in another location, with no visible connection between the two, a field exists between the two objects. Particularizing this statement to electricity, if two flat metallic plates are placed in planes parallel to one another as shown in Figure 19, and are interconnected with a switch and battery, closing the switch causes the center reading ammeter to deflect momentarily and then return to zero. If the

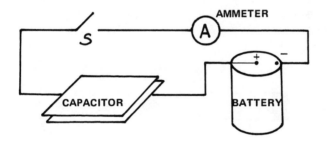

Figure 19. Closing the switch allows electrons to flow to the positive plate. This electron flow deflects the ammeter momentarily.

switch is again opened, and a resistance is connected where the battery was, closing the switch will cause the ammeter to deflect momentarily in the opposite direction. From this observation it appears that what flowed into the plates from the battery, flowed out when the resistance was substituted for the battery. Actually, when the battery was present and the switch closed, electrons were attracted to the plate connected to the positive terminal, leaving positive ions on the plate connected to the negative terminal. When the battery was removed, electric energy was stored between the plates in a static electric field. Once the plates had been charged, the ammeter needle, which had deflected on passage of the electrons, returned to zero again. This rate of movement of electrons is designated as amplitude and the flow of electrons is called an electric current. With the battery removed, the resistance inserted, and the switch closed, the stored electrostatic energy flowed from the plate and was dissipated as heat in the resistance.

Leonhard Euler,* in his *Letters to a German Princess,* written in 1761, pictures a magnet and writes of the "lines of flow of the magnetic fluid." From this description of the magnetic effect in a magnetic circuit, there arose the terms "magnetic flux" and "magnetic flux lines." The substantive nature of the field may be seen. If a compass is brought near a magnet, one end of the compass pointer will be attracted, as demonstrated in Figure 20. If the

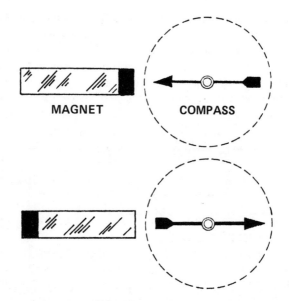

MAGNET   COMPASS

Figure 20. A compass needle is attracted by the North Pole of a permanent magnet and repelled by the South Pole. Courtesy Theodore Audel Co.

direction of the magnet is reversed, the end of the compass pointer formerly attracted will now be repelled. Therefore a magnet affects a compass with its magnetic field, and the direction of the field affects the compass pointer. If

---

*Euler, a broad-gauged scientist and mathematician, completed his *Theory of the Moon's Motion* only after his home had burned, destroying many of his papers. He was blind and carried all the elaborate computations in his head.

a compass is added to the circuit in Figure 19, with the battery in the circuit and the switch opened, as in Figure 21, the compass pointer is unaffected. If, however, the switch is closed as done previously, the compass

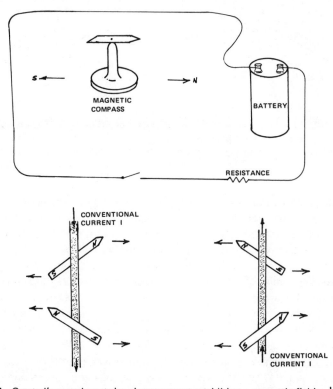

Figure 21. Oersted's experiment showing a current establishes a magnetic field. In the
figure, the wire conductor is aligned north and south. The battery, switch, and current
limiting resistance are as shown. With the switch closed and the current flowing as the
arrow indicates, a compass under the wire will deflect in the way indicated. Likewise
the deflection is shown with the compass above the wire. If the current is reversed
as shown on the right lower drawing, the compass needles will deflect as shown.
In all four cases there are two magnetic fields present: the Earth's magnetic field,
and the magnetic field established by the current flowing in the wire.

pointer is deflected when current flows. Now, with the capacitor charged and
the switch opened, if, as in the first example, the battery is removed and a
resistance put in its place, the compass pointer will be directed in the opposite direction. Affecting the compass is said to be a magnetic flux which is at
right angles and concentric to the current flow in the conductor. Figure 22

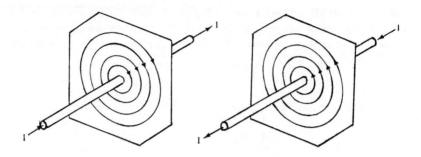

Figure 22. The magnetic field of a straight current-carrying wire. The lines of force are concentric circles in a plane perpendicular to the wire. If the right-hand thumb is in the direction of the current, the fingers are in the direction of the force.

indicates the direction of magnetic lines around a conductor-carrying current where the arrows represent direction of current flow. Note that if with your right hand your thumb is in the direction of current flow, your fingers point in the direction of the flux. This observation will become important in understanding why an electric motor can produce torque. Hans Christian Oersted, the Danish physicist, first observed this effect in 1820. At the time the current flowed in the conductors, a magnetic field was established around the conductors. When the electric field was present, and a current no longer flowing, there was not a magnetic field around the wire. Thus we have the phenomenon of almost instantaneous magnetic field build-up associated with current flow. But when the electrostatic field was established there was no magnetic field. As the electrostatic field disappeared in the second case, the magnetic field appeared as a result of the discharging current. Thus there is an interchange of energy from a magnetic field to an electric field, and like-wise from an electric field to a magnetic field. This oscillation of energy from an electric to a magnetic field is known as dynamic fields.

If a wire is coiled as shown in Figure 23 and a current is passed through the wire, a magnetic field is established threading the axis of the coil in the direction indicated. Using the hand rule, if the fingers are in the direction of the current flow through the wire, the thumb points in the direction of the lines of force. Where those invisible lines of force emerge is known as the north pole of the magnetic field; where they enter is the south pole. If a bar of iron is placed within this coil, the lines of force may be greatly in-creased, by a factor of possibly 500 or more. the iron increases the intensity of the lines. The metal nickel also serves to increase the intensity of these lines. Other than iron or nickel, and their alloys, almost no other materials

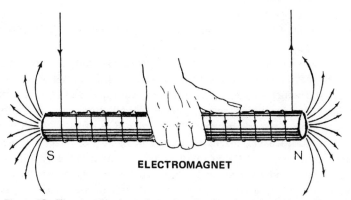

Figure 23. The thumb rule to determine the direction of the North Pole in
an electromagnet. Courtesy Theodore Audel Co.

show such enhancement. As will later be seen, this phenomenon means that
an electric motor or an electric transformer will always contain masses of
iron and copper, the latter serving to conduct electric current.

MAGNETISM

Earlier, when electric and magnetic fields were being illustrated, the concept of a magnet was brought into the discussion to show how its field
affected the pointer of a compass, and to demonstrate how the pointer was
similarly affected by a field surrounding a conductor carrying a current.
Analogously, an electric current in a conductor creates a magnetic field.
What is it in iron and other ferrous materials that allows them to possess
strong magnetic properties, a phenomenon possessed by few other elements,
and then only in a modest degree? Magnetism is thought to be caused by the
unique alignment of the spin axes of all the orbital electrons* of the iron
atoms, these atoms operating in units of magnetic domains. In this scenario,
not only are the electrons orbiting the nucleus, but each is spinning on its
own axis. This representation is not unlike the earth orbiting around the sun
once a year, but spinning on its axis once every 24 hours. The more the
spinning axes of the electrons are aligned, the higher the intensity of the
magnetic field. In nonmagnetic materials spin orientation is random. Sharp
jarring or high heating can cause spin alignments to become less perfect, re-
ducing the effectiveness of the magnet. The Curie Point of a magnet is that
temperature where magnetism disappears. It is usually lower than the melting
point of the ferrous material. For unalloyed iron it is 770°C.

---

*The concept of electron spin was first described by Samuel Goudsmit and G. E.
Uhlenbeck in 1926.

Natural magnets in nature are minerals composed largely of iron oxide possessing a polarity. Such trophies are sometimes called loadstones. Artificial magnets may be permanent or temporary, depending on their ability to retain their magnetic strength after the magnetizing force has been removed. Soft iron and annealed steel readily become demagnetized after the magnetizing force has been removed. Special alloyed materials, when properly heat-treated, have remarkable retention of high flux density. Such magnets are used in loudspeakers, magnetos, meters, magnetrons, telephone receivers and many other devices. Permeability is the term used to describe the ability of material to become magnetized when placed in a magnetic field. The permeability of a material is determined by experiment, based on an arbitrary assumed value of unity for a vacuum. The permeability concept serves the same purpose in the magnetic field as the dielectric constant does in the electric field.

The science and art of fabricating permanent magnets with the desired characteristics has shown a remarkable development. Permeabilities of magnet material can now be had at values over 1,000,000, a figure 300 times greater than what was available at the turn of the century.

ELECTROMOTIVE FORCE AND ELECTRIC CURRENTS

If two dissimilar metals are immersed in a beaker containing a dilute acid solution, and the metals are connected by conductors through an ammeter, the meter will deflect, indicating a passage of current. The word current in electricity is analogous to flow of a fluid in a water pipe. Current is measured in amperes after the Frenchman, Andre Ampere, 1775-1836. (An ampere is the unit of intensity of an electric current produced by one volt acting through a resistance of one ohm.) As current represents a flow of electrons, it is seen that this phenomenon resulted from the presence of an electromotive force known as voltage. The word voltage in electricity corresponds to pressure on a fluid in a water pipe. Voltage is measured in volts after Italian Count Alessandro Volta, 1745-1827. (A volt is the measure of that electromotive force which, when steadily applied to a conductor whose resistance is one ohm, will produce a current of one ampere. An ohm is the unit of resistance of a circuit in which a potential difference of one volt produces a current of one ampere.*)

The metal-acid-beaker assembly is recognized as an electric cell. When two or more cells are connected together they form a battery. Batteries, which

---

*The careful reader will recognize the circuity of the above practical definitions. The *Encyclopaedia Brittannica* gives basic definitions with considerable description under the heading "Electricity."

can supply substantial voltages and currents, are widely used. When a much higher voltage is required, or when large currents are employed, a generator is utilized. The amplitude of the voltage and the current may be represented on a graph. If the voltage is constant and simple elements are present, then the circuit will carry a constant current. If the voltage is periodically interrupted and current flows periodically as a consequence, an intermittent current results. Electric utilities use turbo-generators to produce an alternating voltage resulting in an alternating current (ac).

In Figures 24a, 24b and 24c are examples of constant current (direct current), intermittent current, and alternating current. Amplitudes of the quantities are plotted vertically, while time is represented on the horizontal. The electric vehicle uses all three of these currents: constant current supplying headlamps from the lighting battery, intermittent current from the controller to the motor, and alternating current from the receptacle to the charger when the battery is being replenished.

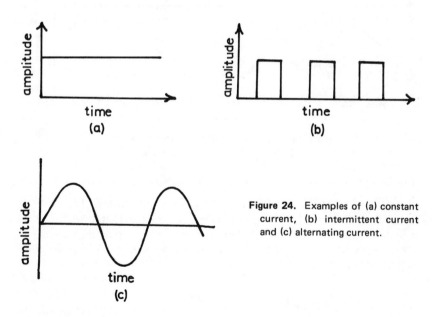

Figure 24. Examples of (a) constant current, (b) intermittent current and (c) alternating current.

FREQUENCY

Frequency has a common occurrence in nature. In harmonic motion it is the number of vibrations per unit time. In music it is pitch. The note A has a frequency of 440 vibrations per second. In electricity, frequency is the number of complete cycles of current or voltage produced by an alternating current generator in one second. Figures 25 and 26 represent currents with a

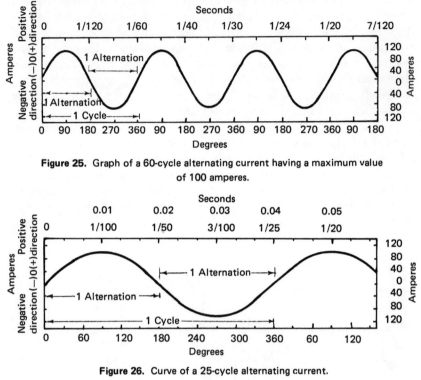

Figure 25. Graph of a 60-cycle alternating current having a maximum value of 100 amperes.

Figure 26. Curve of a 25-cycle alternating current.
Courtesy: McGraw-Hill Book Co.

frequency of 60 cycles and 25 cycles per second, respectively. The time represented from where the rising current crosses the horizontal axis to where it again crosses the same axis is known as the period T of the current. A period is measured in seconds. The inverse of the period T is known as the frequency, f, of the current.

$$\frac{1}{T} = f \text{ in cycles per second (Hertz)}$$

One cycle per second is known as one Hertz (Hz). The utilities supply an alternating current with a frequency of 60 cycles per second, or 60 Hertz. This frequency is maintained with such precision that the hands of an electric clock are driven by a synchronous alternating-current motor. The name given for this frequency comes from German physicist Heinrich Hertz (1857-1894).

RESISTANCE, POWER AND ENERGY

In a given electrical circuit where the only change made is successively modifying the composition of the wire conducting the current, some metals are found to carry current more readily than others. This difference in current-carrying ability is due to the difference in resistance, R, of various metals. The word resistance in electricity corresponds to friction in a water pipe. Resistance is measured in ohms, after German physicist George Ohm (1787-1854). As iron previously was shown to conduct magnetic lines of force more effectively, so some materials carry a current more readily than others. Materials providing little opposition to the flow of electric current are known as conductors, and those offering much opposition to the flow of current are called insulators. As indicated in the section on atoms and electric charge, the electron configuration of the outer shell determines if a material will be a conductor or an insulator.

Conductors		Insulators
metals	dry air	porcelain
carbon	glass	most plastics
acid	wood	rubber

If pure drawn copper wire has a resistance of unity (1.0), then other metals have the relative resistances shown in Table VII.

Table VII. Relative Resistivity of Metals* at 20°C

Aluminum (pure)	1.67
Copper	1.0
Gold	1.45
Graphite	470.0
Iron (pure)	5.9
Lead	13.1
Nickel	4.1
Silver	0.96
Zinc	3.4

*Generally, alloys have a higher resistance than their components.

The resistance of wire, therefore, is seen to depend on its composition. The resistance of a wire also is subject to its length (see Figure 27). One wire twice as long as a piece of the same wire will have twice the resistance. As indicated in Figure 28, wire with a larger cross-section will have a lower resistance than same composition wire with a smaller cross-section. The relationship of resistance to length and cross-section is as shown. The equation

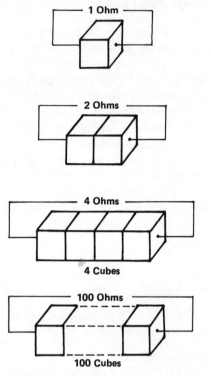

Figure 27. The resistance of a conductor varies with its length.

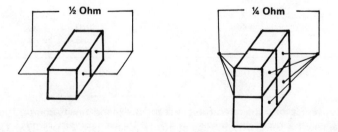

Figure 28. The resistance of a conductor varies with its
cross-sectional area. Courtesy Theodore Audel Co.

reads: resistance (R) is proportional (k) to length (L), and inversely proportional to the cross-section of the conductor.

$$R = k \frac{L}{A}$$

Thus a wire with twice the cross-sectional area of a second wire of the same material will have one-half the resistance of the second wire. The resistance of a copper conductor increases as its temperature rises. Copper is said to have a positive resistance. This increase of resistance with temperature can be a self-limiting action for current. To take an example, the resistance of the tungsten filament in a lamp increases sharply from its resistance at room temperature to its resistance when the lamp is lighted. The resistance of carbon, on the other hand, decreases with increasing temperature. Carbon is said to have a negative temperature coefficient of resistance.

By experiment there is a simple relationship between voltage, E, current, I, and resistance, R.

$$E = I R$$

In this equation voltage is in volts, current is in amperes, and resistance is in ohms. If any two of the elements of the equation are known, the third can be determined. This equation is known as Ohm's Law.[*]

If we have an electric battery and circuit as shown in Figure 29, where A represents an ammeter to measure current, E a voltmeter to measure voltage, then the resistance R can be determined:

$$R = \frac{E}{I}$$

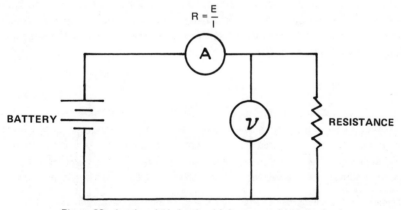

BATTERY

RESISTANCE

Figure 29. An electrical circuit with battery and resistive load, monitored with an ammeter and a voltmeter indicated, can be used to demonstrate Ohm's Law and Watt's Law.

---

[*]Georg Ohm, a German *hochschule* teacher, discovered this relationship between voltage and current in 1827.

The Power, P, flowing from the battery and appearing as heat in the resistance is E multiplied by I. If for E we substitute I R in the above equation, then

$$P = I R \cdot I = I^2 R$$

Therefore, if one knows the value of R in ohms, and the current flowing in amperes, the power dissipated in watts can be determined, where I is in amperes and R is in ohms. A watt is a unit of power. One watt is equal to the product of one ampere and one volt. Power is the rate of doing work. The unit of power was named after the English engineer, James Watt (1736-1819). In electric vehicle usage, a 1000-watt unit is more applicable. A kilowatt is 1000 watts. One kilowatt, kw, is equal to about 1.3 horsepower, hp. It would enable a 4000-pound vehicle to cruise at 6 mph on a level surface.

Energy is the capacity to do work. Energy may be represented as power multiplied by time.

$$Work = energy = power \times time$$
$$= watts \times hours$$
$$= watt\text{-}hours$$

Divide by 1000 and obtain the widely used energy unit, the kilowatt-hour, kwh. It is with this unit of electricity that billings from the electric utilities are calculated. A typical American home might use 8000 kwh of electricity a year. If one kwh is 4¢, the annual electric bill would be $320 per year. In practice, electric rate determination is more complex than the example cited, but the basic principle is illustrated. The kwh electric unit is also useful in electric vehicles. An electric vehicle may use one-half kwh or less per mile of travel. At 3¢ per kwh, the incremental rate, the electrical energy cost for the vehicle is 1½¢ per mile.

CAPACITANCE

With capacitance electric energy may be directly stored without a chemical intermediary such as a battery. When two conducting plates (shown in Figure 19) are separated by an insulating material (the dielectric) such as air they have the ability to store electric energy. Such an assembly of surfaces is known as a capacitor.* The capacity of two surfaces is measured in

---

*Pieter van Musschenbroek of the University of Leyden accidentally discovered the first capacitor. It became known as a Leydon jar. Initially it was a corked glass phial partially filled with water. A long pin pierced the cork and touched the water. Held in the hand, the jar was electrically charged by contacting the pin to a friction machine which separated charges. Otto von Guericke, a German physicist made the first such machine in 1745. Benjamin Franklin in 1752 electrically charged a Leyden jar from lightning with cord and key. Fortunately Franklin was not killed in this experiment, as occurred in the case of G. W. Richman of the Petersburg Academy of Science in 1753.

farads. The word capacity in electricity corresponds to the volume of a water bucket. The word farad is the unit of measurement for that capacity, and derives from the name of the English experimenter, Michael Faraday (1791-1867). Since a farad is a large unit, one millionth of a farad (a microfarad) is a more convenient size.

The capacitor in Figure 19 has a capacitance of one farad when the electromotive force (emf) across the plates is varying at one volt per second when one ampere is flowing. The amount of energy that can be stored in a capacitor is proportional to the area of the surfaces, and inversely proportional to their separation. The closer the two surfaces, the more energy that can be placed within the capacitor until limited by puncture of the dielectric. The type of insulating material between the plates also has a bearing on the energy stored. Two plates separated by mica will store 5.2 times more energy than the same plates separated by air. This energy storage improvement factor is known as the dielectric constant of the separator. Mica has a dielectric constant of 5.2.

For a capacitor, the capacity C, the area of its plates A, their separation d, and the dielectric constant ϵ of the separator are interrelated by the equation:

$$C = \frac{A}{d}\epsilon$$

Some commonly used insulators and their dielectric constants are:

| air | 1.0 | glass | 4.7 |
| mica filler | 5.2 | nylon | 3.5 |

In manufacturing, to obtain large capacity, capacitors have surfaces of aluminum foil separated by wax paper. This assembly resembles a sandwich rolled into a spool from which emerge two conducting leads. If too high a voltage is placed across a capacitor, the insulator will be punctured and the capacitor rendered useless.

The electrical charge q, which can be stored in a capacitor is dependent on the capacity C and on the impressed voltage E

$$q = C \cdot E$$

where q is in coulombs,* C is in farads, and E is in volts across the capacitor. The word coulomb comes from French physicist Charles Augustin de Coulomb (1736-1806). An ampere of current flows in a conductor when it is carrying one coulomb per second. A coulomb is also the quantity of

---

*Nobel Laureate Robert Andrews Millikan with his "oil drop experiment" found the value of an electronic charge to be 1.60×10^{-19} coulombs. As this value is the charge of an electron, the quantity of electricity in one coulomb is the reciprocal, $1/(1.60 \times 10^{-19}) = 6.24 \times 10^{18}$ electrons, equal to the figure above. The precision of this number is known to greater accuracy than is the population of a large city.

electricity on the positive plate of a capacitor of one farad capacity when the electromotive force is one volt. As a coulomb represents 6243 quadrillion electrons, if that many electrons passed a given point in a conductor in one second, one ampere of current would be flowing in that conductor.

In the section on electric fields, we had a direct current voltage placed across a capacitor and the current surged with closing of the switch, then reduced to zero, and surged when a resistance replaced the battery and the switch was again closed. So may a capacity be placed across an alternating voltage, as in Figure 30. The alternating current can alternately charge the

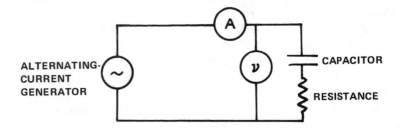

Figure 30. An alternating-current circuit with capacitive and resistive load.
A variation of Ohm's Law is applicable in this circuit.

the capacitance positively and negatively. An alternating-current meter will read this flow of current, with the pointer remaining steady. In this case the meter reads the root mean square (RMS) of the current, and the root mean square of the voltage, where the impressed wave form is a sine wave as illustrated in Figure 25. The RMS of an alternating current is that measure of an alternating current which has the same heating effect provided by a direct current of equivalent amplitude.

INDUCTANCE

When energy is transferred to a magnetic field, the work is accomplished by an electromotive force. Power is required to perform this work. As earlier stated, Power = E · I. The power previously referred to and associated with resistance is known as resistance power, while the power required to create a magnetic field is known as inductive reactive power. Resistance power, once expended, is forever lost, appearing as heat. Reactive power, on the other hand, with collapse of the magnetic field, is returned to the circuit. The voltage of the reactive power represents the opposing voltage induced in the circuit when the magnetic field is increasing to its final value. When this magnetic field reaches its final value, the back emf is zero. Thus, in this field building process, the back emf opposed the source voltage, resulting in a slower rise in current than expected. Now the amplitude of this back emf is proportional to the rate of rise of the current, and is characteristic of the circuit itself. This characteristic or constant is indicated as the inductance, L, of the circuit. Its unit of measurement is the henry (h), named after the American physicist Joseph Henry (1797-1878). An inductor is said to have an inductance of one henry if an emf of 1 volt, induced in the inductor, is changing at the rate of 1 ampere per second. Mathematically this definition is expressed as

$$E = \frac{L \, \Delta I}{\Delta t}$$

where E is the induced emf in volts, L is the inductance in henrys, and ΔI is the change in current in amperes occurring in Δt seconds. This effect is expressed in Lenz's Law[*]: The induced emf in any circuit is always in a direction to opposite the effect that produced it. The mechanical analogy of inductance is mass. The mechanical force required to accelerate a body is the product of mass and acceleration. Anyone who has attempted to push an automobile knows the difficulty of getting the car moving, but once underway it seems easier to keep it going. Figure 31 provides examples of magnetic induction.

The inductance of a circuit depends not only upon the physical characteristics of the conductor, but the material associated with the circuit itself. If the conductor is in the form of a coil the polarity of the induced emf is always in the direction which opposes the change in current. Consequently, if the current were to decrease and the stored magnetic energy were to flow to another section of the circuit, a counter emf would be induced which would limit this flow of current. The inductance of a circuit, therefore, serves to smooth the flow of an intermittent current. This smoothing action can be further enhanced by inserting iron within the conductor soil cited above. Such action, by increasing the intensity of the magnetic field, can enhance the inductance of a circuit as much as 1000 times. An example of this smoothing action in electric vehicle circuits is seen in the battery current. With a chopper controller providing an intermittent current to the motor, viewed on an oscilloscope screen, the current actually is observed to be scalloped rather than in square pulses. This departure of the current trace from the intermittent square wave voltage trace of Figure 28 is due to the inductance of the power circuit of the vehicle.

SERIES AND PARALLEL CONNECTIONS

In the preceding section on resistance, we observed that if a wire is made twice as long as its original length, its resistance would be doubled. In a

---

[*]H. F. E. Lenz (1804-1865) was a contemporary of André Ampere and Hans Christian Oersted.

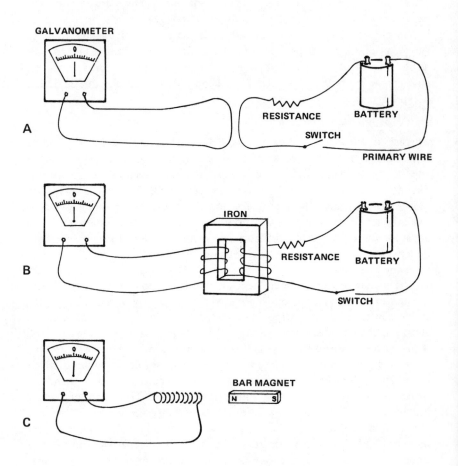

Figure 31. Faraday's experiments on induction.

A. When the switch is closed the galvanometer deflects momentarily and returns to zero when steady state current flows in the primary.

B. When the switch is closed the galvanometer deflects momentarily and over a greater arc. The iron has intensified the flux linkage.

C. A bar magnet introduced into a hollow coil of wire connected as shown will deflect the galvanometer.

sense, the second length of wire was thus placed in series with the first section. When the cross-section of the wire was increased, we saw that a like section of wire may have been placed in parallel with the original piece.

Therefore, electric circuits, including circuits in electric vehicles, contain instances of series and parallel connections.

Electrical elements are said to be in series when the current is flowing through one element, and all of the same current (or flux, in the case of a magnetic circuit) subsequently passes through the second element. Electrical elements are in parallel if an electric current (or flux), when approaching two or more electrical elements, is divided, parts flowing through the various elements simultaneously. Figures 32 and 33 are common electrical elements in series and in parallel connections, respectively. As unique elements standing

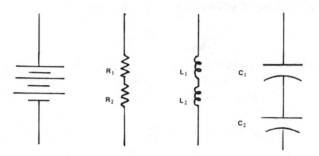

Figure 32. Examples of electrical elements connected in series. From left to right: batteries, resistances, inductances and capacitors.

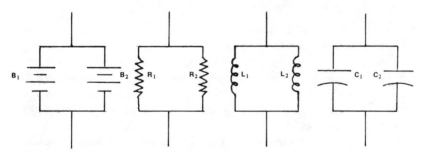

Figure 33. Examples of electrical elements connected in parallel. From left to right: batteries, resistances, inductances and capacitors.

alone, inductances and capacitances would be used as separate elements only in alternating current circuits, or in circuits where the current is varying. The operator of an electric vehicle or his mechanic would seldom have occasion to touch or manipulate connecting electric elements, with the exception of the batteries, and these only after several years of operation. Consequently, we shall discuss first the motive power batteries and the voltage batteries add when placed in series.

Many electric vehicles are a nominal 72-volt system. Since each cell has a nominal voltage of 2 volts, there are thirty-six cells in series. Many electric vehicles use elements of 6-volt batteries, each 72-volt string of batteries consisting of twelve batteries connected in series. If twelve 6-volt batteries were connected in parallel, the system would be a 6-volt system, but capable of supplying twelve times the current as compared to the series connection.

For resistance in series,

$$R_{series} = R_1 + R_2$$

If R_1 = 2 ohms, and R_2 = 3 ohms, then R_{series} = 5 ohms. Resistances add when placed in series. And when resistances are in parallel,

$$\frac{1}{R_{parallel}} = \frac{1}{R_1} + \frac{1}{R_2}$$

Solving, using as the least common denominator, $R_1 \, R_2$

$$\frac{1}{R_{parallel}} = \frac{R_2 + R_1}{R_1 \, R_2}$$

$$R_{parallel} = \frac{R_1 \, R_2}{R_1 + R_2}$$

In the parallel connection, using the same values as above for R_1 and R_2,

$$R_{parallel} = \frac{(2)\,(3)}{2+3} = \frac{6}{5} = 1.2 \text{ ohms}$$

So, with the same resistances placed in parallel, the resulting resistance is less than when the same resistances are in series.

In the case of inductance, when in series, and in an alternating current circuit, the inductances add as do the resistances above. When in parallel, the inductances are treated mathematically the same as the resistances. In other words, the inductance of a circuit is less when elements are in parallel than when they are in series.

With capacitors, the capacitance of a circuit is increased when the capacitors are in parallel. As shown in Figure 33,

$$C_{parallel} = C_1 + C_2$$

When capacitors are in series, they are treated the same as resistances in parallel,

$$C_{series} = \frac{C_1 \, C_2}{C_1 + C_2}$$

Capacitors in series yield less capacitance than when in parallel.

In the case of electric vehicles, the motive power batteries will almost always be found connected in series. Because each battery has a small internal resistance, the resistances add, since the elements, like the batteries, are in series. Each battery also possesses a capacity, and these capacitances too will be in series. But as stated earlier, the driver of an electric vehicle will rarely need to have a mechanic change any connections, except the batteries, and those infrequently.

POWER FACTOR

The term power factor was used in the section on standardization of receptacles. It was said that since the battery charger was both a resistive and an inductive load, the current for a given power would be greater than if it were a resistive load only. As will be seen in Chapter 3, a battery charger typically includes a transformer. A transformer contains iron and is inductive. With a two-trace oscilloscope, if an operator placed one input to the instrument across the two input wires connecting the electrical receptacle to the charger, and the other input in series with the charger, two sine wave traces would be observed. One, first crossing the horizontal axis furthest to the left of the tube face, would be the voltage trace, while the one to the right would be the current trace, as in Figure 34.

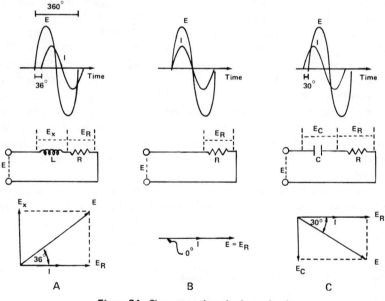

Figure 34. Shown are three basic ac circuits-
Circuit A is inductive-reactive. The current lags the voltage by $36°$. Its power factor is the cosine of $36°$, or 0.81.
Circuit B is resistive. The current is in phase with the voltage. Its power factor is the cosine of $0°$, or 1.0.
Circuit C is capacitve-reactive. The current leads the voltage by $30°$. Its power factor is the cosine of $30°$, or 0.86.

If a large capacitor were placed across the input to the charger, the trace for the current, which we agreed was lagging the voltage, would be seen to lead the voltage. Earlier we saw that one cycle represented 360 degrees. If one cycle represents 360°, then before the capacitor was inserted, possibly the picture on the oscilloscope screen showed the current lagging the voltage by a tenth of a cycle or 36°. And when the capacitor was placed in the circuit, the current led the voltage by a twelfth of a cycle, or 30°. If the trace of the current and the voltage cross the horizontal line at the same point, the current and voltage are said to be in phase. That would be representative of a pure resistive load. The angle would be zero. And the cosine* of a zero angle is 1, or unity. The cosine of 36° is 0.81. The cosine of 30° is 0.86. The cosine of an angle is always one or less, and the cosine of the angle between the current and the voltage is the power factor of the circuit. Figure 34 illustrates these three examples.

The power placed in the battery, omitting charger losses, is the product of the receptacle voltage, the current and the power factor. If that power factor were 0.50, the power company would be like the merchant who had 50% of his goods returned. To encourage the customer to have a high power factor, one near unity, an electrical utility is permitted to charge the customer more if his power factor is too removed from unity. Referring to the section on standardization of receptacles, the demand was 4 kw, or 4000 watts. With $P = EI$ cosine θ, if P remains 4000, and E remains 230 volts, and if the power factor of the battery charger is 0.81, then I must be larger. A reactive load, like a battery charger, requires greater current than does a resistive load; and in the illustration we did increase the current. If we set standards in 1977 for electric vehicles not yet conceived, we know that if they are charged at 230 volts, a generous electrical service must be provided. So we have settled on 230 volts, 50 amperes. This is the same service provided for electrical ranges in homes.

In the next section losses in transformers will be discussed, followed by an explanation of how a transformer works. Remember that nearly every charger contains a transformer, and a typical home commonly may contain as many as ten.

EDDY CURRENTS AND HYSTERESIS

If a coil surrounds iron as demonstrated in Figure 23, and if the current is changing in the coil, an emf will be induced in the iron. Since iron is a conductor, although a poor one compared with copper, current will flow in the

---

*In a triangle, the cosine of an angle is the ratio of the length of the adjacent side to the length of the hypotenuse. The ratio is one or less.

iron. The iron has resistance, and there will be a power loss (an $I^2 R$ loss) in it. This loss is due to the flow of eddy currents. Eddy currents are found in the laminations of the insulating transformer of the battery charger. They are found in both the armature and stator laminations of the vehicle's electric motor. This loss, present when the circuits are actuated, is minimized by making the transformer and the motor of silicon steel laminations. Each sheet bears an insulating material to limit the flow of current from one lamination to another. Figure 35 demonstrates how laminating an iron core reduces eddy current losses.

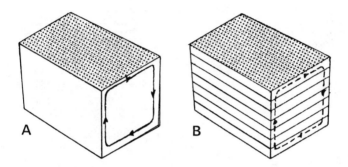

Figure 35. If the magnetic flux-carrying iron core is made of steel laminations rather than solid iron, eddy current losses are reduced. a) Solid iron. b) Steel laminations. Courtesy Theodore Audel Co.

The iron, subject to this ever-changing electric and magnetic field, is observed to dissipate power through the phenomenon known as hysteresis. A name first given by Scottish engineer and physicist J. A. Ewing in 1890, it describes the rotation and the change in volume within minute magnetic domains of the iron. Like eddy current, hysteresis represents a small loss in all elements of the vehicle drive system (where the voltage is changing rapidly and where there is iron) totalling probably 1-2% of the complete power handled. Such losses together with the energy loss appearing in the current-carrying conductors in both the controller and motor cause these bodies to heat. After the electric vehicle has been driven perhaps an hour, the outside frame of the motor will be warm to the touch.

THE TRANSFORMER

An electric vehicle may contain a transformer in the on-board charger. Such an element could be required because the voltage at the receptacle is 120 volts, while the vehicle may have a 72-volt battery system. A transformer is an electrical device with no moving parts, which transfers alternating-current electric power by electromagnetic induction from one circuit to another circuit, usually to a different voltage, without a change in frequency. The principle of the transformer was first recognized by Michael Faraday in his experiments on electromagnetic induction. Transformers are widely used and are among the prime reasons for the almost universal application of ac power in all parts of the world.

To understand the operation of a transformer, reference should be made to Figure 36. Here there are two windings of insulated wire surrounding a

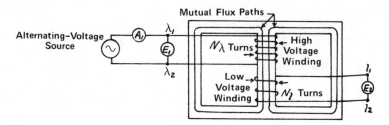

Figure 36. Windings and connections fo a simple transformer.

central magnetic core constructed of sheet steel laminations to reduce the losses from eddy currents and from hysteresis. In the figure, an alternating voltage, with a wave form as shown in Figure 25, is applied to terminals h_1 and h_2 of a winding having N_h turns. This winding is known as the primary winding. The application of an alternating voltage to the primary winding initiates an alternating magnetomotive force that establishes an alternating magnetic flux in the steel core. The alternating flux induces a back emf of self-induction in the primary which limits the current flow to a greater extent than the resistance.

When there is no load on the secondary winding, the small current flowing in the primary winding is known as the exciting current of the transformer. With the assumption that the magnetic flux in the core is the same through both the primary and secondary windings, the voltage induced in each turn is the same in both windings. As a result, the voltage as measured with the voltmeter V_1 at the primary, bears a relation to the voltage on the secondary V_2 directly as the turn ratio of the respective windings. Neglecting transformer losses, which are small, one may say:

$$\text{Power into primary} = \text{Power out of secondary}$$
$$\text{as Power} = E\,I$$
$$E_1\,I_1 = E_2\,I_2$$

where the subscripts 1 and 2 represent primary and secondary windings, respectively. As a transformer is usually employed either to increase or decrease voltage in an electrical circuit, then by example, if E_1 is twice E_2, I_2 is twice I_1. Stated in words: In a transformer, the voltage varies directly with the turns ratio, while the current varies inversely with the turns ratio.

Large transformers employed by the electric utility industry have efficiencies as high as 98%. Smaller transformers that may be used in the battery charger of an electric vehicle will have efficiencies of 85-95%. A transformer in its lack of moving parts, its great utility, its high efficiency, and its constant availability is a poem of elegance in design. To make efficiency measurements on transformers and other electrical equipment, tests are performed using instruments. The next section discusses some of the most useful types of test instruments for electric vehicles.

ELECTRICAL INDICATING METERS FOR ELECTRIC CARS

Electrical phenomena may be the easiest to measure, since facilities can be readily devised to move an indicator that can be seen and read. Useful in testing the drive train of an electric car are the ammeter, the voltmeter and the ohmmeter. Highly developed for measuring the energy placed in the battery of a car is the watt-hour meter. Readings from this instrument form the basis of electric billing today. All of these instruments are quite common, but their principles of operation are less well known.

The Ammeter, the Voltmeter and the Ohmmeter

The three most useful portable meters for an electric vehicle are the ammeter, the voltmeter and the ohmmeter. Typically, the voltmeter for ac and dc use is in a case bearing multiple scales. The most useful scale to match the measurement may be selected by a switch. A dc ammeter usually will be a separate instrument. In all three measurements of current, voltage, and resistance, the deflecting needle is driven by a current flowing in a magnetic field, as illustrated in Figure 37. An instrument utilizing this principle is known as a D'Arsonval* type meter. When measuring a voltage, for example, the switch on the meter (Figure 37) is set to the applicable scale. Current enters one probe and passes through a calibrated resistance within the meter. Motor action deflects the bobbin against a control spring. Where the needle rests, a number may be read on the dial indicating the voltage of the circuit at the point measured.

---

*Jacques D'Arsonval (1851-1940) was a French physicist who developed the galvanometer which bears his name. He conducted extensive experiments with high-frequency currents in therapeutic applications.

SCALE CALIBRATED IN VOLTS

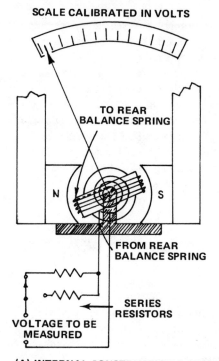

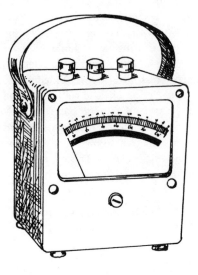

(A) INTERNAL CONSTRUCTION & CIRCUIT   **(B) EXTERNAL VIEW**

Figure 37. Simplified D'Arsonval voltmeter circuit.
Courtesy: U.S. Navy Bureau of Personnel.

With the meter used as an ohmmeter, place an internal battery, already encased in the box, in the circuit by the selection switch. Before making a resistance measurement, adjust the selection switch to the desired scale. Null your instrument by bringing the two leads together in contact. If the meter fails to read zero (with the leads together there is zero resistance between them), use the adjust knob. If it still fails to read zero, a new battery may be required. With the meter nulled, a resistance reading can be made.

The most common method of measuring a current is to use an ammeter. In an electric vehicle where many of the currents are large, the major share of the current flows through a shunt of known resistance. A small portion of the total current flows through the meter to deflect the needle. The meter is calibrated, when properly used, to measure current in amperes in the circuit. The use of the shunt is shown in Figure 38. A more detailed study of the shunt is displayed in the same figure.

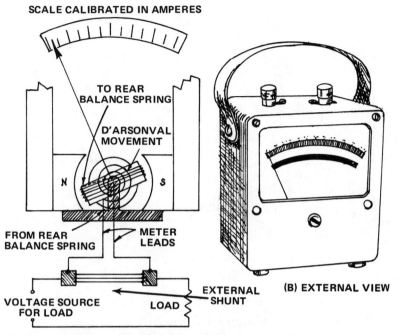

SCALE CALIBRATED IN AMPERES

TO REAR
BALANCE SPRING

D'ARSONVAL
MOVEMENT

N   S

FROM REAR
BALANCE SPRING

METER
LEADS

VOLTAGE SOURCE
FOR LOAD

LOAD

EXTERNAL
SHUNT

(B) EXTERNAL VIEW

(A) INTERNAL CONSTRUCTION & CIRCUIT

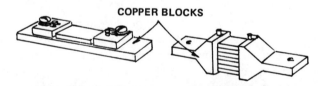

COPPER BLOCKS

(C) TYPICAL EXTERNAL AMMETER SHUNTS

Figure 38. Weston ammeter employing D'Arsonval principle in its movement.
Courtesy: U.S. Navy Bureau of Personnel.

The Watt-Hour Meter (Induction Motor Type)

The energy delivered to an electric car is measured by a watt-hour meter.
The kilowatt-hour readings from this meter are periodically recorded by personnel from the electric utility and form the basis of the electric bill. With
the aid of Figure 39, the operation of the instrument is more readily followed. The electric supply enters from the left as an alternating current.
Passing to the right, the lower conductors carry the ac load current which
induces a magnetic field in the iron core around which it is coiled (the current
coils in the diagram). This field is proportional to the load current. On the

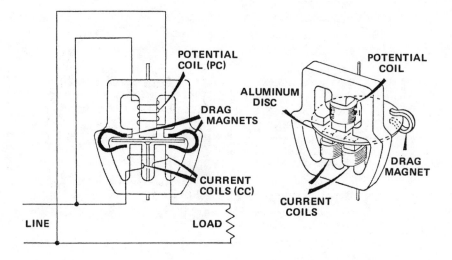

(A) CIRCUIT ARRANGEMENT (B) PHANTOM VIEW

Figure 39. Simplified sketch of an induction watt-hour meter.
Courtesy: U.S. Navy Bureau of Personnel.

left, conductors also branch from the supply line in parallel with the load.
The ac current in this line, the potential coil, remains tiny because there are
many turns of small wire around the iron core. This current is highly inductive and, as a consequence, has a large phase angle between itself and the current flowing through the load. In the air gap between the magnet pole faces
is an aluminum disc. The induced alternating magnetic field in the iron
induces eddy currents in the disc. Because of the phase angle between the
currents of the two conducting circuits, in the air gap and disc, forces appear
which cause the disc to rotate.* Serving to damp this rotation are drag magnets, which may be positioned to adjust the meter reading.

The speed of rotation of the disc is dependent on the two currents. The
upper one is a measure of voltage, V, across the load. The lower one is a
measure of the current, I, through the load. The product of these two
parameters is power, P = V I, and represents the speed of rotation of the disc.

---

*The principle of induction led to the invention in 1888 of the induction motor by the
Hungarian, Nickola Tesla, 1856-1943. The induction motor runs the factories of the
world, and a form of it runs electric wall clocks. The elegance and simplicity of design,
low cost, and modest maintenance have, together with the transformer, made ac power
dominant in the world.

The number of turns of the disc is a measure of energy. Through gearing, the aluminum disc causes dials to rotate on the watt-hour meter face which may be read from left to right as kilowatt-hours. The dial hands must always be read for the figure last passed, and not the one approaching. With the cooperation of the electric utility company, the reader interested in maintaining a record of the energy consumed only by his vehicle, can have such a watt-hour meter installed especially for his vehicle.

IMPORTANCE OF WAVE FORMS IN MEASUREMENTS

In modern electric vehicles a chopper type controller serves to limit the current flow to the motor. The output current from the chopper fed to the motor is a succession of square pulses with a forward spike. Most meters have been designed to read either steady-state current or alternating current. The chopper requires the battery to deliver pulsed intermittent current. The wave shape of this current is further modified by the inductance of the total circuit. As steady-state, intermittent current and alternating current all affect the meter differently, the readings obtained will only be approximations. Hence caution is indicated in measuring current with an ammeter in a circuit containing a chopper. Wave form, affecting meter results, has an impact on calculation of the efficiency of electrical vehicle elements as well as other electrical elements. Efficiency is discussed in the following section.

EFFICIENCY

An early section of this book referred to the high efficiency of the electric power train. It was said to have an efficiency of 75-85%. What is the meaning of efficiency? Efficiency can be either a ratio of two powers, or of two energies, and is associated with the rate of doing work, or work itself. Efficiency is a ratio of output to input, expressed, output/input. This ratio is always less than one and is expressed in percent. If 12 kwh are delivered by the batteries, and only 10 kwh reach the wheels, the drive system has an efficiency of 10/12 = 83%. Efficiency is abbreviated eff.

$$\text{Efficiency} = \text{eff} = \frac{\text{output}}{\text{input}} = \frac{\text{input - losses}}{\text{input}} = \frac{\text{output}}{\text{output + losses}}$$

To make the concept of efficiency part of the real world, losses in a dc motor for a high-performance electric vehicle are categorized as follows:

1. Mechanical losses
   a) Bearing friction loss
   b) Windage, or air resistance
   c) Commutation friction loss

    2. Copper or I^2R losses
       a) Shunt field copper loss
       b) Armature circuit loss
       c) Brush contact loss
    3. Core or iron loss
       a) Hysteresis loss
       b) Eddy current loss

Such a motor would have a full-load efficiency of 87-90%. Total losses are 10-15%. The comparabe efficiency for an IC engine is 15-20%, with losses of 80-85%. The electrical element for which the efficiency measurement was made was probably protected from destruction by a fuse, the next subject.

FUSES

An often small but always necessary element in an electrical circuit is the fuse. A fuse is a link in the electric circuit. If the current becomes greater than that for which the circuit components were designed, the fuse link heats and melts. This action opens the circuit, and current flow halts. The remaining elements in the circuit, often expensive or necessary for safety, are thus protected from damage. The battery charger described below has a current protective fuse in its circuit. Figure 40 illustrates cartridge-type fuses, while Figure 41 shows the fuse link which melts. Some fuses are replaced entirely; in others only a fuse link is restored. After a fuse has been found blown in a circuit, the cause of the excessive current must be determined

Figure 40. The dual-element fuse is designed to pass current (not open) on harmless surges, such as motor starting, etc., while reacting quickly to short circuits or dangerous or prolonged overload. Courtesy: Bussmann Mfg. Co.

Figure 41. Typical renewable fuses.
Courtesy: Bussmann Manufacturing Co.

and the indicated repair made, before placing the circuit again in operation. The fuse must be replaced with one of the same current rating, which will be marked on the body of the fuse. Following this sequence, power may be safely applied to the circuit.

Basic electricity has been discussed; the ammeter, voltmeter, ohmmeter and fuses have been described. Let us now portray the principal components of an electric vehicle other than the chassis and the body. We start with the charger. This module is the first element on the electric vehicle that accepts energy from the electric utility company lines. From the charger, current flows through the battery and back to the charger and finally to the utility mains. Once the charger has been disconnected from the electrical receptacle, current flows from the battery through the circuit breaker, to the controller, to the motor, and finally, after work has been done, all the current returns to the battery, but at a lower voltage than when it left the battery. In an entirely separate electric circuit, current can flow from the lighting battery through the actuating mechanisms of the windshield wipers, horn and headlamps, and back to the battery. The following pages will make the electric vehicle and its modules more understandable.

REFERENCES

1. Stebbings, Ronald F. "High Rydberg Atoms: Newcomer to the Atomic Physics Scene," *Science*, 193(4253) (1976).

CHAPTER 3

THE ELECTRIC VEHICLE

"If you continue to make your present caliber of automobile, and I my present quality of battery, the gasoline buggies will be out of existence in no time."

> Thomas Alva Edison to Walter C. Baker, President of the Baker Motor Vehicle Co. of Cleveland, in 1902.

"In fifteen years more, more electricity will be sold for electric vehicles than for light."

> Thomas Alva Edison in 1910. The year 1925 saw the production of a few thousand electric vehicles and 3,733,171 gasoline-powered cars.

A well-designed and maintained electric vehicle will be a faithful servant in fair weather and foul. Our discussion of the elements in the electric car will follow the order in which power is delivered to them successively from the wall-mounted receptacle where electric utility-generated power awaits. From the receptacle, the power flows, in order, to the battery charger, the motive power battery, the magnetic contactor, the controller, and finally to the motor where electric power is converted into mechanical power that moves the vehicle. For convenience, the accessory battery for lighting, the windshield wiper, etc., are described in the section on batteries.

Figure 42 is a photograph of the power train modules appearing under the hood of a modern high-performance electric vehicle. The front of the vehicle is directed toward the reader. At the lower left is the coiled electric power cord. This cable transmits ac power from the electric receptacle to the charger which converts ac power to dc power. The charger is the module on which the meter and timer are located. The ammeter reads the dc current entering the batteries. The timer enables the operator to schedule the period over which he wishes to charge the battery. From the charger the power flows to the motive power batteries. Power flows from the battery to the solid-state controller, seen as the module on the lower right. On the right side

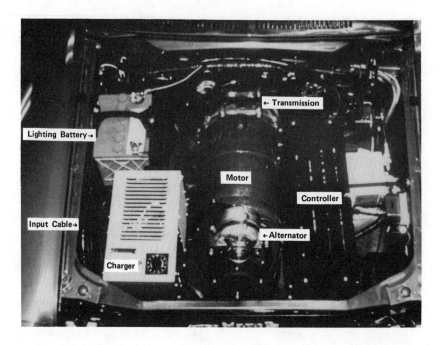

Figure 42. An illustration of the electrical modules under the front hood of a modern high-performance electric vehicle. Shown is the input cable, the charger, the controller, the motor, the alternator and the auxiliary battery. Courtesy: Linear Alpha, Inc.

of the controller can be seen the cable linking the accelerator pedal and the controller. From the controller, electric power, in the vehicle shown, is delivered in electrical pulses to the dc electric motor, which occupies the center of the picture. Changing electrical power to mechanical power, the motor delivers power to the transmission of the vehicle. The transmission housing appears in the upper center of the illustration. In the foreground, mounted on the motor, is an alternator, belt-driven from the motor shaft, which serves to charge through a rectifier the 12-volt auxiliary battery seen in the upper left. This picture should help the reader visualize the component elements of the vehicle.

THE BATTERY CHARGER

A battery charger should be aboard an electric vehicle unless the vehicle has a specialized application. An on-board charger greatly enhances the flexibility of the vehicle and minimizes the chance of the driver and his passengers being stranded. A battery charger accepts alternating current from an electrical outlet and converts it into direct current at the voltage required by the battery. This charging current reverses the chemical reaction that occurred in the battery during discharge. A quality charger is also designed to deliver current to the battery at a rate required for this chemical reaction. A greater current rate may cause electrolysis of the battery electrolyte, chemically disassociating water into hydrogen and oxygen gases, a phenomenon known as gassing. Gassing signifies an excessively high charging current and necessitates more frequent watering of the batteries. In addition, unless the charger limits the flow of current as the chemical process is completed, the batteries may overheat, shortening their life. A quality charger, therefore, tailors the current flow to the needs of the batteries to which it is connected.

Battery chargers can be of two classes: the isolated type, or the nonisolated type. In the former, a transformer magnetic field links the alternating current at the power outlet with the rectifying circuit of the charger. A nonisolated-type charger omits this magnetic link. In current rectification, the positive lobe appearing on one end of the transformer secondary in the charging circuit of Figure 43 is permitted to pass into the battery. The positive

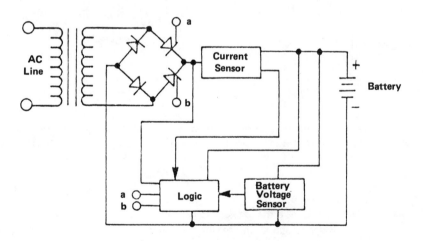

Figure 43. A circuit diagram of a battery charging circuit with constant current and a voltage-sensing cutoff. From left to right are the isolating transformer, a full-wave rectifier, and circuits which control current and voltage supplied to the battery being charged. Courtesy: Gould Inc.

lobe appearing on the other end of the secondary is also allowed to flow into the battery, in both cases by unidirectional diode action. Thus the current through the battery is always unidirectional. The higher-quality chargers also permit, to the rectifying circuit, a smoothing or filtering circuit (consisting of a capacitor, not shown in the figure) which serves to cause the current flow into the battery to be more uniform with time. Figure 44 (a-d) illustrates voltage wave forms from the 120-volt receptacle as it proceeds through the charger to the battery. Figure 44a is the ac voltage at the receptacle. Notice

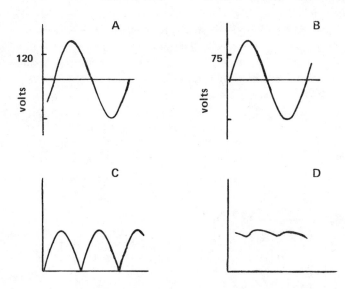

Figure 44. Diagram of wave forms (a) out of receptacle into transformer, (b) out of transformer into rectifier, (c) output from full-wave rectifier, and (d) the wave-form smoothed at the output of the capacitor. This final tailored dc voltage is applied to the battery, but only after it has been regulated by the current sensor and the battery voltage sensor.

that 120 voltages is not the peak voltage. It is what is known as the root mean square, RMS, which, with the sine wave voltage generated by the utility industry, is 0.707 the value of the peak voltage. The output voltage of the transformer, in the case illustrated, Figure 44b, is a lower ac voltage, 75 volts. Observe that the wave form is the same; only the amplitude is reduced. At the output of the full-wave rectifier, the negative lobe of Figure 44c has been rectified giving two positive lobes. This wave form is now a pulsating dc voltage, now "tailored" for charging the battery. The information above follows the wave form illustrations, while the description in the next paragraph follows the circuit diagram, Figure 43.

In describing the operation of a battery charger, reference is made to Figure 43, a schematic diagram of an isolating charger. To the left of the figure is a transformer which changes the magnitude of the input voltage to that value required by the full-wave rectifier, the diamond-shaped circuit. The full-wave rectifier is a solid-state circuit whose input is an ac voltage and whose output is a dc voltage, which may be further shaped by capacitors to provide a smoothed input voltage to the battery. Limiting current flow into the battery is the function of the current sensor. If too much current is provided, the current sensor signals the logic to act on points a and b, limiting current to the battery. Likewise if too small a current were flowing to the battery, more current would be permitted to flow. As a battery charges, each cell rises from a lower to a higher voltage, going from the right in Figure 45

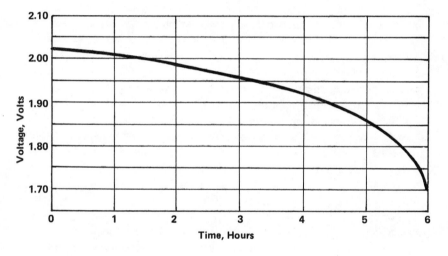

Figure 45. Motive power cell. Typical voltage profile when charged at 6-hour rate at 77°F. Courtesy: Gould Inc.

and following the voltage line to the left of the diagram. A fully charged cell has a voltage held by a regulator to 2.35 volts. If the high-performance vehicle were a 54-cell system, the battery would be fully charged with 54 times 2.35, or 126.9 volts. As the battery system voltage approaches this upper limit, the battery voltage sensor indicates to the logic that the charging current should be gradually reduced to only a taper charging rate of 2-3 amperes. If the above is followed, the vehicle battery system will provide optimum service.

Most important in proper use of the charger is that it be connected to a power outlet at the voltage for which the charger was designed. Avoid an unregulated utility circuit, which by State Commission Regulation is allowed to have a change of voltage of ±10%. Some chargers may not be designed for such a variation in applied voltage, and trouble could be experienced by the vehicle operator in a frequent need to replace protective fuses in the charger. To conclude, the charger for an electric vehicle needs to be carefully projected. It must match the voltage and the current from the electrical receptacle to the voltage and acceptance current of the battery at all states of charge. Only with a properly built charger, integrally part of the vehicle's system design, can the operator assure maximum life and efficiency of the battery.

ELECTRIC STORAGE BATTERIES*

An electric battery is two or more cells each of which has the ability to induce a chemical reaction between two dissimilar materials to produce a flow of electric current. There are two general classes of batteries: primary and secondary. A primary battery provides a system for conversion of chemical energy directly into electric energy. It requires replacement of the exhausted chemical constituents to return to its original condition. A primary battery is usually discarded after a single exhaustion. A flashlight battery is a primary battery, as are the batteries placed in hand-held calculators. A secondary battery, on the other hand, accumulates a useful amount of electric energy by means of a reversible chemical reaction, and can repeatedly be charged and discharged. Electric vehicles use secondary batteries for energy storage.

A storage battery is a remarkable source of energy. It can deliver large amounts of power instantly without noise, fumes, poisonous gases or unforeseen breakdown. The delivered electric power is easily transported where required. And the power can be readily converted into mechanical energy, light, heat or sound. It can also supply heavy overloads for short periods. In his study[1] of batteries for electric vehicles, Sidney Gross stated that they should have the following characteristics:

1. High energy density
2. Low manufacturing cost
3. Long life with low maintenance

*The first electric battery, assembled by the Italian physicist, Count Alessandro Volta in 1800, was a primary battery. It consisted of a series of silver discs (the cathode), a disc of cloth saturated with a salt solution (the electrolyte), a disc of zinc (the anode); then a silver disc in dry contact with the zinc, followed by an electrolyte layer and a second zinc disc, and so on. Substantial voltage could be obtained. This discovery enabled Sir Humphry Davy to isolate alkali metals, and to invent the carbon arc lamp, and led to further discoveries by Davy and others.

4. Low self-discharge when not in use
5. High power rate for acceleration
6. Efficiently and quickly recharged
7. Small size
8. Safety in accidents
9. Readily available
10. Little special equipment required for handling the batteries.

The only commercial batteries qualifying these respects are the lead-acid[*] type batteries, which have been gradually improved for more than a century since their invention. The closer this battery is examined, the better it appears for electric vehicle application. Gross, in his excellent review on batteries for transportation, thinks that during the next five years, the lead-acid battery will bear the rating "excellent," and even over a 15-year span, he rates it as attractive as more exotic batteries, earning in this time period the rating "good."

MOTIVE POWER BATTERIES

A pod of motive power batteries is shown in Figure 46. This source of stored electrical energy provides power to the controller and motor. These batteries are connected in series and provide power at a nominal 156 volts.

The modern lead-acid battery consists of a lightweight, nearly unbreakable polypropylene case filled with dilute sulfuric acid in which positive and negative plates are immersed. The negative plate contains sponge lead within an antimony-lead grid. The positive plate has a similar grid bearing lead dioxide. On discharge of the positive plate, the lead dioxide becomes lead sulfate; and the sponge lead of the negative plate becomes lead sulfate, and releases hydrogen gas. As can be seen from the chemical reaction on discharge, lead, lead dioxide, and sulfuric acid are consumed, with lead sulfate and water produced. The maximum number of ampere-hours, the product of current and time, is governed by the weights of the active materials. When a charging current is forced through a battery in the opposite direction from current flow of discharge, the chemical reaction converts the lead sulfate and water to lead dioxide and lead and releases sulfuric acid into the solution again. On discharge, the electrolyte is seen to have a greater share of water; and, since water has a lower density than sulfuric acid, a hydrometer is used to determine the condition of battery charge. The information contained in Figure 47 and Figure 48 makes clearer the operation of a lead-acid battery.

---

[*]The lead-acid couple as a battery was first implemented by Gaston Planté in 1859, who rolled up two long sheets of lead separated, it is said, by his wife's petticoat, and placed the assembly in dilute sulfuric acid. In 1881, Camille Faure devised the lead grid and lead paste assembly currently used. Since then there have been constant small improvements.

Figure 46. A pod of motive power batteries in an electric vehicle. The van is shown in Figure 60. Courtesy: Linear Alpha, Inc.

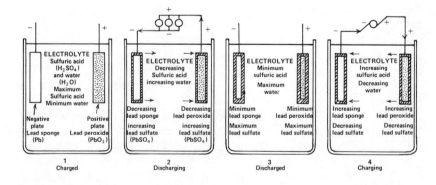

Figure 47. Chemical action in a cell on cycle of discharge and charge. Courtesy: McGraw-Hill Book Co.

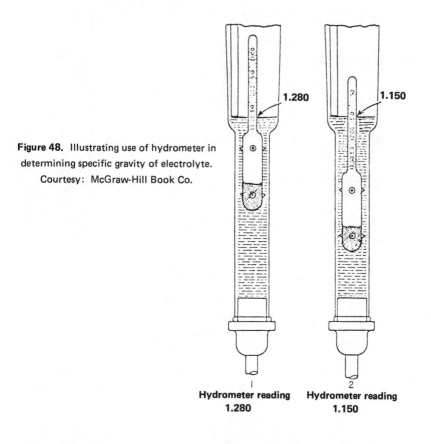

1.280   1.150

Figure 48. Illustrating use of hydrometer in determining specific gravity of electrolyte. Courtesy: McGraw-Hill Book Co.

1
Hydrometer reading
1.280

2
Hydrometer reading
1.150

The attainable energy density of a lead-acid battery is dependent on the discharge rate of the battery as illustrated in Figure 49. For electric vehicles, a duration of 1-2 hours should be considered applicable. The limitation is that on discharge of the battery lead sulfate is deposited on the surface and pores of the electrodes. This action reduces the surface area remaining for the chemical reaction, and also reduces pore size, thus limiting the access of the electrolyte. In addition, the sulfuric acid of the electrolyte becomes depleted within the confines of the pores. The sum of these actions serves to reduce the available energy from a battery at high discharge rates. A 220 ampere-hour battery is commonly used in electric vehicles. This rating derives from the measurement that the battery is capable of continuously providing 11 amperes for 20 hours. In the literature, the 20-hour rate may be only implied. Since electric vehicles require much higher current in their usual operation, the ampere-hour rating should be based on a shorter period.

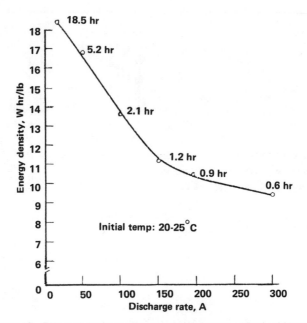

Figure 49. Effect of discharge rate on energy density of lead-acid batteries.
Courtesy: Pergamon Press.

The capacity of the battery, being a function of discharge rate, is also affected by the fact that the battery is temperature-dependent (as shown in Figure 50). Capacity at rapid discharge is limited by the rate at which the sulfate ion diffuses to the reaction site on the electrode surface. At high currents, ion depletion results proceed with greater speed, giving lower capacities. If, after such a high rate of battery discharge, the vehicle is halted for a short while, and the ions are permitted to diffuse to the reaction sites, additional energy may be obtained from the battery. An electric vehicle driver with experience will have observed this phenemon.

With the battery at a low temperature, the viscosity of the electrolyte increases. This feature also slows the diffusion rate. In addition the electrolyte resistance is increased, limiting power delivery. Hence the effect of low temperature on the battery is to limit the capacity of the battery. Figure 50 demonstrates the capacity of a motive power battery as a percentage of its capacity at a 6-hour discharge rate versus the temperature. It is apparent from the illustration that as the temperature is lowered, so is battery capacity. The detrimental results of environmentally low temperature, however, can be minimized by garaging the vehicle so it does not "soak" for days at low temperature. If it were to soak, be certain the batteries are fully charged,

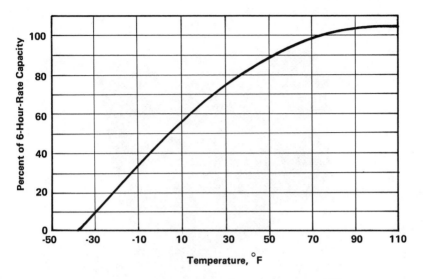

Figure 50. Motive power battery. Capacity as a percentage of 6-hour rate. Capacity *vs.* temperature. Courtesy: Gould Inc.

because at such time, a greater share of the electrolyte is sulfuric acid. Also limiting negative effects of temperature is the normal operation of the vehicle. With operation, the batteries heat due to internal resistance. With charging, the batteries heat for the same reason. In addition there is the mass of the batteries, quite different from the ignition batteries on IC vehicles. Finally, note that the electrolyte is largely water, and water is one of the most difficult substances to change temperature because of its high heat capacity, 30 times more than mercury. For these reasons, temperature problems with electric vehicle operation in Chicago have not been severe.

Batteries in an electric vehicle should be treated with respect. In modern electric vehicle design, batteries are outside the passenger compartment and hence separated from passengers in the event of collision. Modern electric cars are advancing to higher voltage battery systems ranging from 72 to 156 volts. The greater the curb weight of the vehicle, generally the higher the voltage.

The most common energy storage system is the lead-acid type, and will remain so for some years. Thus more detail is devoted to it. The lead-acid battery may be of the industrial or quasi-industrial type, but more readily available are 6- or 12-volt series of cells connected by cable to provide voltage for the specific power desired, the current demanded, and the energy capacity sought to meet vehicle specifications. In Figure 51, the construction details of a lead-acid battery are shown.

Figure 51. A lead-acid cell. Courtesy: Gould Inc.

A. All new container material: Container and one piece cover are made of polypropylene—a super-tough, space-age plastic unaffected by acid, gasoline, motor oil, antifreeze, hydraulic fluids, solvents, and temperatures to 250° F. Walls, only 1/4 as thick as hard rubber, yet have 20 times the impact strength at 0°F. Container and cover are fused together under heat and pressure, become one solid, inseparable piece of plastic.

B. More plates: Stronger, thin walls allow 12% more inside space for additional plates, bigger plates, and up to a pint more acid. Results in faster cranking, more total cranking power, and greater reserve capacity than in same size hard rubber batteries.

C. Hi-torque construction: All cell connections are made straight through the partition walls. Shortens the power path—reduces internal resistance. Results in greater power efficiency and higher terminal voltage.

Vehicles possessing speeds for expressways will, in general, have a higher operating voltage than those vehicles designed for transport only on secondary roads. The greater power required at higher speeds, due primarily to the negative drag of windage, necessitates either more voltage and current, or more of both, since the product of voltage and current equals power. From the equation $P = EI$, where P is power, E is voltage applied to the motor, and I is the current to the motor, if P is increased, E or I or both must increase. A greater current requires a larger diameter cable and, in the case of controls, a more expensive control element. With electric vehicles, as opposed to internal combustion vehicles, it is more convenient to employ electric terms rather than mechanical definitions. Hence in power requirements, as an example, one speaks of kilowatts rather than horsepower, and "motor" rather than "engine." The index and a conversion table at the end of this book can be helpful in better understanding these terms.

THE AUXILIARY ELECTRICAL SYSTEM
AND METHOD OF CHARGE

An auxiliary electrical system is necessary for an electric car, just as it is for the IC vehicle, and has been developing for more than a century. Because the 12-volt ignition battery is standard on cars, parts for such a system are readily available. With these ingredients commonly obtainable, electric vehicle manufacturers also employ a 12-volt system for lighting, as well as operation of the windshield wipers and horn on their vehicles.

The electric vehicle manufacturer has three choices for sustaining a charged 12-volt battery: He may charge the 12-volt battery from the same charger which provides energy to the motive power battery, employing a second output, for 12 volts, from the charger. He may charge the 12-volt battery from the motive power battery by a step-down oscillatory circuit. Or he may equip the vehicle with an alternator, as are IC cars, utilizing a belt-drive power pick-off from the motor shaft. In the first case, care must be exercised in charger design so that both the motive power and the lighting battery can received a tapered charge when required. In the second case, the step-down oscillating circuit must be generously designed to handle substantial currents yet provide for a taper charge of the 12-volt battery. In the third case, the alternator must be adjusted so that in normal vehicle operation the 12-volt lighting battery is always maintained with sufficient energy to provide safe driving lights.

DETERMINING THE INTERNAL RESISTANCE OF A BATTERY

To determine the internal resistance of a battery, operate at full load for ½ hour. Measure the voltage, noting the current. Open the circuit and immediately measure the voltage before depolarization takes place. The no-load voltage will be higher than the full-load voltage. Using Ohm's law:

$$R_b = \frac{E_{n_1} - E_{f_1}}{I_{f_1}}$$

Where R_b is battery resistance, E_{n_1} is no-load voltage, E_{f_1} is full-load voltage, and I_{f_1} is full-load current.

The internal resistance of satisfactory vehicle batteries should be inherently small. A vehicle battery must have a low resistance, otherwise it would overheat quickly. For example, using an earlier equation:

$$P = I^2 R$$

As seen from the cruising power graph for an electric van, the power required for 40 mph cruising is about 25 kw = 25,000 watts. These vans are known to have a battery voltage of about 150 volts.

As $P = E I$

$$I = \frac{P}{E} = \frac{25000}{150} = 167 \text{ amperes}$$

now from above $P = I^2 R$

Since $I = 167$, the square of this number is very large. Thus R in ohms will need to be very small to obtain an acceptable amount of power in watts to be dissipated within the battery.

CARE OF BATTERIES

The manufacturer of the electric vehicle will have selected the size of cable for the electric current flowing through the batteries and their interconnects. He also will have considered safety precautions in both the location and tie down of these energy containers, as well as the electric contacts. For safety, the terminals of a battery system should be completely enclosed, so that the terminals can be reached only through the use of a tool. This safety concept should apply no matter from which direction the battery is approached, even from the underside with a wire. The manufacturer, before making the interconnect cables, if such are required, should have coated the metal surfaces with Zappon, then secured the cable lug contact. Such care allows ready flow of electric current, and inhibits the formation of lead oxide crystals, often seen on battery terminals and identified by their light blue color. If such material appears and a poor electric contact is believed present, the battery circuit should be opened at a clean terminal, with a suitable insulated tool. Next the circuit should be opened at the suspected poor contact, carefully wiping the crystals free using sandpaper if necessary. All contacts should be cleaned, all metal surfaces sprayed with Zappon, and contacts that were opened earlier snugly replaced. The battery surfaces should always be kept clean for best results.

While a hydrometer may be used to determine the amount of charge in a battery, the electric vehicle operator soon learns from the difference in vehicle acceleration whether his battery is fully charged, and if it isn't, its state of charge. The experienced electric vehicle driver rarely employs a hydrometer to determine the specific gravity of the battery electrolyte. The rapid acceleration obtained with a fully charged battery gradually degrades with time and use. The operator comes to recognize how often the batteries need water to keep the active surface plates covered with the electrolyte. Every 6-8 weeks in normal driving is usual, with a properly tapering charger. If there is an overflow of the electrolyte when the battery is watered, the sur- face should be wiped dry with a clean dry cloth. Care must be taken that fingers do not contact the bare electrical elements or the acid-wet cloth.

From the batteries, the current flows to the magnetic contactor which is discussed next.

THE MAGNETIC CONTACTOR

A magnetic contactor is an electrical switch operated by an electromagnet. It may be placed in the electrical loop of an electric vehicle (EV) as a safety- interrupt-device. When the EV is not operating, the magnetic contactor is open and no current flows in or from the battery. At such times the vehicle is immobile by self power. Figure 52 illustrates a magnetic contactor. It is made from a stationary electric magnet, denoted as *a* in the figure, a movable

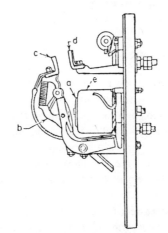

Figure 52. Magnetic contactor.
Courtesy: Square D Company

iron armature *b*, on which is mounted an electrical contact *c*, and a station- ary electrical contact *d*. When there is no current flowing through the operating coil of the electric magnet *a*, the armature is held free from the magnet by means of a spring. Under such conditions, contacts *c* and *d* are open. When the coil is energized, however, the magnet attracts the armature and closes the electrical contacts *c* and *d*.

To close a magnetic contactor and thus make the vehicle operable, electric vehicle manufacturers have two choices: (1) a magnetic relay may close the contactor and make the vehicle operative by turning on the ignition key, or (2) the vehicle may be made operable by closing in sequence the ignition key and depressing the accelerator pedal. When initiated by the ignition key, the 12-volt battery is the source of current closing the relay of the magnetic contactor. When operated by the accelerator pedal, the motive power battery is the source of energy. In both cases there must be electric energy available to close the relay. To have this energy available when wanted, the batteries must be maintained in a charged condition. In the gasoline-powered vehicle, the analogy is to have a tank containing gasoline. The circuit closed by the magnetic coupler may contain considerable energy in magnetic fields due to the relatively high inductance of the circuit. Normal opening of the magnetic contactor without a suppressing circuit could cause undue sparking at the contactor and consequent short life for its contacts. A free wheeling diode may be placed in the circuit to enable this stored energy to be harmlessly dissipated.

With the contactor closed, current from the battery may pass to the controller. Because the controller establishes the speed and acceleration of the vehicle, much attention must be given to it. In addition it is the electrical module in the car with which the uninitiated is least acquainted and probably has the most questions about.

THE CONTROLLER

While the driver of the electric vehicle is varying the position of the accelerator pedal in accordance with driving conditions, he is controlling the flow of power to the motor. In all electric motors of any size, at the start there must be a current limit to avoid burning out motor windings. This controller may be simple or complex. For a lightweight golf cart, the controller might be only a resistance electrically inserted between battery and motor; or switching of batteries might be arranged so that at the start, a relatively low voltage is impressed upon the motor. In both instances, current is limited at start-up of the motor by application of Ohm's Law. With the motor gaining speed, there is an automatic self-limiting current action, known as back electromotive force, generated within the motor which serves to limit current flow. The initial current-limiting device may be completely withdrawn from the circuit as speed is gained.

With modern electric vehicles stressing range, at start-up the trend is to use a control device known as a chopper. As its name implies, this solid-state control device chops the power from the battery into discrete time blocks (energy bundles). A lightly depressed accelerator pedal provides relatively widely spaced bundles of energy. A deeply depressed pedal provides periods of longer, more closely spaced power flow. A vehicle equipped with a chopper will yield a characteristic whine on acceleration, for the same scientific reason that a transformer in your home hums. The rapidly changing current flow into the motor resulting from the pulsed voltage output of the chopper provides a rapidly varying magnetic field. The steel of the motor, laminated to minimize eddy current and hysteresis losses, carrying the magnetic flux, is affected by this field. The hum results from the silicon steel laminations vibrating against each other. This sound is known as magnetostrictive noise. When the speed of the vehicle reaches approximately 30 mph, the voltage pulses from the chopper are timed together so closely, and the laminations have such reduced vibrations that the hum becomes imperceptible. The chopper adds substantially to the cost of the vehicle.

Direct current motor controls from the simplest to the more sophisticated are: (1) temporary insertion of a resistance in series with the armature to limit current flow, as shown in Figure 53; (2) variation of battery voltage

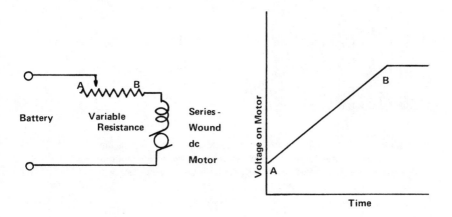

Figure 53. Armature current is resistance-limited.

across the motor armature, obtained by battery switching, illustrated in Figure 54; (3) the combination of resistance insert and voltage switching; and (4) the use of a solid-state chopper where the average voltage presented to the motor is reduced on starting by a time control of pulses. Figure 55 is a representation of this method.

Resistance Type (Control Method 1)

The resistance type controller has the advantages of simplicity and low cost and is seen in electric golf carts, a low-performance use. The inserted

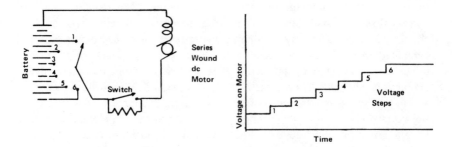

Figure 54. Armature current is voltage-limited.

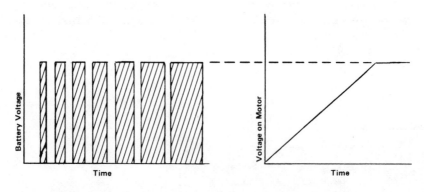

Figure 55. With chopper control, the armature current is voltage limited by the "average" voltage available. The average is increasing in amplitude as one proceeds from left to right in both diagrams.

resistance limits the initial current by the equation $I = V/(R_a + R_i)$, where I is current to the motor, V is applied battery voltage, R_a is resistance of the motor armature, and R_i is the value of the inserted resistance. V is in volts, I is in amperes and R is in ohms. The disadvantage of this method is the loss of energy dissipated in the inserted resistance. It represents energy lost from the battery, which in turn decreases the range of the vehicle. In driving a vehicle of greater curb weight, this loss in range can be prohibitive. Thus high-performance electric vehicles rarely use this method of current control. To appreciate fully the inappropriateness of a resistance control in a high-performance vehicle, let us illustrate by numbers. Suppose, to protect the insulation on the motor and to give a desired acceleration, we wish to limit the current through the motor to 50 amperes. Since R_a, the resistance of the armature, is small, in the calculation it may be neglected. The above equation then becomes

$$I = \frac{V}{R_i}$$

then

$$R_i = \frac{V}{I} = \frac{108}{50} = 2.16 \text{ ohms}$$

Now the power dissipated in this resistance would be

$$P = I^2 R$$
$$= 50^2 \times 2.16$$
$$= 5400 \text{ watts} = 5.4 \text{ kw}$$

In speed control of the vehicle, this resistance (and it would need to be variable) would always be an integral part of the circuit, except at full speed, and would always be dissipating power. On a high-performance vehicle such a design is unacceptable.

Voltage Switching Type (Control Method 2)

While voltage switching is not as simple as the resistance type control, voltage switching is still a reasonably inexpensive means of limiting start-up current to a motor, depending on the number of contactors employed. The starting current to the motor is limited by the application of a low initial voltage being impressed on the motor contacts. Under such conditions the initial current is limited only by the low armature resistance. As the rotor gains in speed, successively higher back emf is generated in the armature serving to limit the current. As the acceleration pedal is despressed further, a successively higher voltage from the battery assembly is switched on until finally the full voltage from the batteries is impressed on the motor. The disadvantage of the voltage switching system for current limitation can be the somewhat jerky acceleration of the vehicle, the clicking sound as the interlocks close, and the maintenance associated with good operation of the interlocks. In addition, there is always the latent possibility of battery voltage imbalance, almost inherent with voltage switching. This imbalance can cause uneven battery life, or the presence of unequally charged batteries in the set.

Voltage Switching and Resistance Insert Type (Control Method 3)

Voltage switching and resistance insert is a technique combining both of the above features. While it is more complex than either of the above methods, the current to the motor is better controlled. Not only is there step application of voltage, but between the steps there is resistance insert. This combination of control yields a smooth start. The disadvantages are described in the two methods above.

Solid-State Chopper Controller (Control Method 4)

The solid-state chopper limits initial current to the motor primarily by the time duration of the impressed battery voltage across the motor. This segmenting of the constant voltage from the battery is achieved by the use of a solid-state element known as a silicon controlled rectifier (SCR).* This SCR acts as a nonmoving electronic switch, turning the battery voltage to the motor on and off in a controlled manner. When the accelerator pedal is initially depressed, there are rather few narrow pulses per second impressed on the motor, as shown in Figure 55. Such a distribution of pulses applies to the motor a low average voltage, which provides the motor with amplitude-limited current. In addition, current is limited by the phenomenon of induction described in the section on basic electricity. As the accelerator pedal is further depressed, the number of pulses per second increases, and the time duration of the individual pulses also increases, yielding an ever higher average voltage to the motor. In addition, as the armature of the motor is gaining in speed, the back emf is increasing. The chopper, therefore, by varying the pulses per second and their time duration, effectively limits the current to the motor. Moreover the control is continuously variable, eliminating the voltage steps present in either resistance limit, voltage switching, or a combination of the two. The chopper is much more efficient than the resistance insert type. It is as efficient as voltage switching, but, possessing no moving parts, is highly reliable. Furthermore, voltage switching can lead to battery unbalance. At full load, the chopper has an efficiency of 95-97%. In some electric vehicles, the chopper is always in the circuit; in others, the chopper element may be removed at full speed.

Figures 53, 54 and 55 illustrate the methods of current limitation. The four methods of control described above effectively limit current through the motor by controlling the average voltage applied to the motor. The speed of the vehicle is regulated to the amount permissible by armature current control. While the natural speed of the motor is a function of motor design, an increase in speed range for a compound type motor can be achieved by varying the current in the shunt field. If the current in the field windings is decreased by a controller, the armature speed increases to build up the back

---

*The SCR was invented by Dr. Nick Holonyak, now Professor of Electrical Engineering at the University of Illinois. It is a child of the remarkable array of solid-state devices ushered in with the discovery of the transistor by William B. Shockley, John Bardeen, and Walter Brattain for which the three received the 1956 Nobel Price in Physics.

emf generated by the conductors of the armature cutting a reduced magnetic field. This control of current in both the armature and the field windings represents the most complex motor control method cited here. While greater speed range is possible under these conditions, so is the electronic control circuit more complex.

Lightweight vehicles such as golf carts generally employ the control cited in Method 1. Intermediate size vehicles may utilize Methods 1 or 2. Larger, heavier vehicles, and those designed for expressways may prefer Methods 3 or 4. The price of controls increases from Method 1 through Method 4.

In the flow of power through the vehicle, we pass from the control circuit to the motor. In the next section, motors are discussed.

THE ELECTRIC MOTOR

An electric motor converts electric power into mechanical power. With the possible exception of electric lamps, it may be the most common technological device in use today. Its principle of operation was discovered by Michael Faraday in 1831. Electric motors are of two general types: Alternating current (ac) motors and direct current (dc) motors. Nearly all household motors on fans, air-conditioners, washing machines, spin dryers, oil furnaces, etc., are ac motors. An ac motor is inexpensive and operates directly from the ac power supplied by the utility. They are essentially constant-speed. To apply them to vehicles with varying speed requires complex and expensive controls. For that reason, passenger over-the-road electric vehicles will probably use dc motors for some time. The cutaway drawing in Figure 56 illustrates a dc motor.

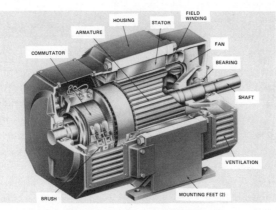

Figure 56. A cutaway section of a dc motor showing the outer frame and stator with its poles and field coils, the rotor including the commutator, brushes and brush housings. Rotation of an electric motor may be conceptually beautiful, but its design and manufacture can be technologically complex. Courtesy: Reliance Electric Co.

An electric motor converts electric power first into a mechanical force. It then develops power by means of rotary motion. In the process torque, or turning action, is involved as well as revolutions per minute at which the torque is made available. As work (W) is a product of force (F) and distance (s), W = F s. Work may be stated in foot-pounds. Power is the rate of doing work. It may be expressed as the quotient of work and time (T), P = W/T. The power of an electric motor is expressed in horsepower or in kilowatts, which can be a derivative of the former. One horsepower is the power required to raise a weight of 33,000 pounds one foot in one minute. The horsepower of a motor is determined from the torque and the revolutions per minute of the motor. Let the shaft of the motor be equipped with a wheel. With the radius (r) of the wheel of one foot, the distance around the wheel is its circumference, and the circumference of a circle is twice the radius multiplied by π. (π is the ratio of the circumference of a circle to its diameter, and has a value of approximately 3.14.) To find horsepower:

$$\text{As } W = F\ s, \text{ and } P = \frac{W}{t}, \text{ and } s = \text{rpm} \times \text{circumference of wheel}$$

$$\text{Then} \qquad P = \frac{F\ s}{t}$$

$$\text{By substitution} \qquad = \frac{F\ \text{rpm}\ 2\pi\ r}{t} \text{ and } t \text{ is } 1$$

$$\text{Horsepower} = \frac{F\ r\ \text{rpm}\ 2\pi}{33,000}$$

As torque is the product of force and the length of the lever arm, and in this case the lever arm is the radius of the wheel, r

$$\text{horsepower} = \frac{\text{torque} \times \text{revolution per minute} \times 2 \times 3.14}{33,000}$$

The horsepower of an electric motor is actually measured in a laboratory using the above formula, with the motor running at several different speeds, by force on a lever arm from the motor shaft by a device known as a Prony brake.[*]

There are two ways to describe torque or turning action developed in a motor. One is the word description below, and the other is seen by following Figures 57 through 59. Each presents torque in a different way, and this helps explain why early 19th century scientists such as Faraday, Oersted and Davy were puzzled until Faraday at last built a motor. A motor may be

---

[*]Baron de Prony (1755-1839) devised a friction brake in which the pull on the flywheel friction blocks is measured by a weighted lever.

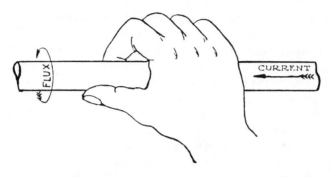

Figure 57. Showing relation of flux and current in a conductor.
Courtesy: Theodore Audel & Co.

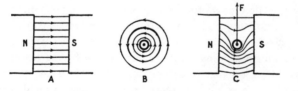

Figure 58. With magnetic polarity shown, current in the conductor directed out of the paper, the force on the conductor is upward. Courtesy: McGraw-Hill Book Co.

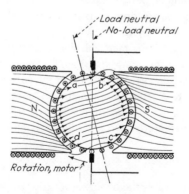

Figure 59. The conductors on the left will experience an upward force. Those on the right will encounter a downward force. The force couple will cause the armature to rotate clockwise. Courtesy: McGraw-Hill Book Co.

described as two magnets: One is fixed and has the visible poles with a flux polarity established by the field windings, as shown in Figure 59. The second magnet is in the rotor. One might think the two magnets would become aligned, with north pole to south pole, and the rotation would cease. Here is the importance of the brushes and the commutator. The brushes serve to introduce current through the commutator bars to an oncoming rotor coil so that the rotor magnet never approaches the stator magnet. The current is continually shifted to the next oncoming coil by means of the commutator. Figure 56 shows the commutator bars and how each is separated and insulated by mica from the adjacent bar. The graphite brushes slipping over the bars continually feed current to the proper coil, providing the continuous rotational force known as torque.

In an electric vehicle the manufacturer may use a series motor, a shunt motor or a compound motor. All are dc motors. The manufacturer will have reasons for his choice. The vehicles shown in Chapter 1 (Figures 1, 2, 5 and 8) are all equipped with series-wound dc motors. Reference to the motor text will provide the advantages and disadvantages of each type motor. A well designed dc motor will usually have a full load efficiency of 85-90% at rated voltage. The type motor used can have a bearing on whether the vehicle contains a transmission. A transmission is a gear system which, in an electric vehicle, enables high initial acceleration with moderate current draw from the battery. Inasmuch as a manual transmission may have a power loss of from 5-10%, and an automatic shift even more, the electric vehicle manufacturer may choose not to employ a transmission, relying on highly efficient electronic controls. In the latter case, the electric motor essentially is connected directly to the drive wheels, with perhaps a differential between motor and wheels, again depending on design. Clearly, the designer of an electric vehicle has more parameters for freedom in planning than does the designer of an internal combustion vehicle system.

While an electric motor is mechanically much simpler than an internal combustion (IC) engine, the operation of an IC engine, because of familiarity, is better understood by the general public and the automobile mechanic. Just as the mechanic had to master the IC engine, so must he become more familiar with the electric drive system of the electric vehicle. To that end he should read and understand the text and drawings below.

Torque Equation of a Motor

Since the electric motor is the direct source of torque for the wheels of the car, it is necessary to understand why electric current from a battery when applied to a motor causes the drive shaft to rotate. The reader will recall that the turning action of a rotor within a motor was explained by the reaction of two magnets. Here it is explained by the force acting on a current-carrying conductor existing in a magnetic field. Reference to Figure 57 indicates that if a conductor is carrying a current, the magnetic field established by the current is directed as shown. This direction relationship is known as the Right Hand Rule. As you cup your right hand, if the current in the conductor travels in the direction of your thumb, the magnetic field set up by the current flow is in the direction of your fingers. Now in Figure 58, the intensity of the flux is increased under the conductor, forcing it upward. Assume now that the same conductor is placed in a slot of an armature of an electric motor, and that the current through the conductor with a dot represents the point of an arrow, indicating the current flow is toward the reader as illustrated in Figure 59. Under such conditions the armature will be forced to rotate clockwise with a force F. The product of force F and radius r is torque T.

$$T = F\,r$$

To achieve continuous rotation of the shaft, when conductor #1 arrives under the north pole, the current flow would need to be out of the paper, as indicated by the Right Hand Rule. So as the conductor moves from the north pole to the south pole, the current through a conductor must be reversed. It is the commutator of the motor which reverses the current so that there is continuous rotation of the armature, and hence the drive shaft of the vehicle. Torque to wheels in Figure 60 is from a series-wound dc motor.

Figure 60. LinearVan powered by series-wound dc motor. Courtesy: Linear Alpha, Inc.

While Figures 58 and 59 explain the principle of operation of a dc motor for electric vehicles, in practice the magnetic flux arises from a coil of wire which slips over the pole piece. The magnetic field set up by this assembly is proportional to the current in the coil multiplied by the number of turns of wire about the pole piece. This product is known as ampere-turns. The concept of ampere-turns is diagrammed in Figure 61. The magnetic flux through a coil is proportional to the ampere-turns and factor k, which is a constant

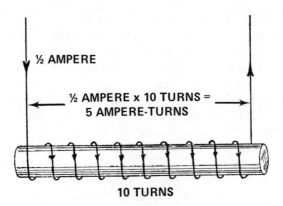

½ AMPERE

**½ AMPERE x 10 TURNS =
5 AMPERE-TURNS**

10 TURNS

Figure 61. Illustrating the meaning of ampere-turns. By definition, the ampere-turns are equal to the product of the current passing through a coil multiplied by the number of turns in the coil. Thus, for example, ½ ampere x 10 turns = 5 ampere-turns. Courtesy: Theodore Audel & Co.

as long as the iron pole piece is not saturated.[*] This equation may be expressed

$$\text{Magnetic flux, } \phi = \text{constant, } k \quad \text{turns, } N, \cdot \text{amperes, } I_n$$

$$\phi = k\, N\, I_n$$

Now the force f on a conductor in Figure 58 is proportional to the magnetic flux and the current in the conductor. Expressed in an equation this is

$$F = K_1\, \phi\, I$$

As

$$T = F\, r$$

then

$$= K\, \phi\, I$$

This equation is the basic torque equation of a dc electric motor. It says that the torque of a motor is the product of a constant, K, the flux, ϕ, and the current, I.

Speed Equation of a Motor

Earlier it was shown why an armature of a motor rotated. What determines speed? If a motor is running, the back emf is always a little less than

[*]The magnetic flux passing through a pole piece is proportional to the ampere-turns until saturation of the iron ensues. As the ampere-turns are continually multiplied, the flux increases ever more slowly until, with saturation, even as the ampere-turns are further enhanced, essentially the flux remains constant.

the applied emf, the difference being the voltage drop in the armature, $I_a R_a$, where I_a is the armature current, and R_a, the armature circuit resistance, including the series field. So

$$E_b = E_a - I_a R_a$$

where E_b is back emf, and E_a is applied voltage at the armature. Now E_b will be proportional to the flux per pole, and the rpm of the armature. This relationship may be expressed as

$$E_b = K \phi \text{ rpm, where K is a constant.}$$

Therefore,

$$\text{rpm} = \frac{E_b}{K\phi}$$

By substituting

$$\text{rpm} = \frac{E_a - I_a R_a}{K\phi}$$

This statement becomes the basic speed equation for a dc electric motor. It says that the speed of a motor is dependent on the armature voltage, E_a, minus the voltage drop in the armature, $I_a R_a$, divided by the product of a constant, K, and the flux, ϕ, per pole. Controlling E_a and the magnetic flux, ϕ, are the two common means of varying speed.

SERIES-WOUND DC MOTOR

The series-wound dc motor is one of the most widely used motors in electric vehicles, because it has characteristics particularly applicable to traction use. Its high starting torque and its simplicity make it attractive. With the two basic equations in hand for an electric motor: torque and speed, Figure 62 is the symbolic representation for a series motor. Notice that the current

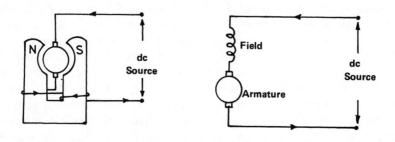

Figure 62. A series-wound dc motor has its armature winding, field coils, and external circuit connected in series with each other so that the same current flows through all parts of the circuit.

from the battery passes through the field coils directly to the armature and back to the battery. Figure 62 makes clear the principle of a series-wound dc motor. Referring to Diagram I, the current from the battery enters the motor at the positive terminal threading the field poles as shown. Remembering the Right Hand Rule, with the thumb in the direction of the current, as the arrows indicate, the fingers point in the direction of the flux lines. The direction of the flux is into the south pole and out of the north pole.

Inspecting the torque equation

$$T = K \phi I$$

As flux ϕ is dependent on current in a series motor

$$T = K I^2$$

which reads that torque is dependent on the current squared. If the current doubles, the torque quadruples. A series motor has a high starting torque. Because of this feature, a manufacturer of electric vehicles, if he chooses, may omit a transmission. A review of the speed equation modified for a series motor, where R_f is resistance of the field winding

$$rpm = \frac{E_a - I_a(R_a + R_f)}{K \phi}$$

indicates that if I_a is changed, there will be a substantial change in rpm, because flux ϕ also is dependent on I_a. With theory and a clearer grasp of the series motor in mind, if the operator depresses the accelerator pedal, what happens? A voltage is placed across the motor. The starting current flows through the field coils on the way to the armature, providing a strong field flux. Combined with the large current in the armature, there is a strong starting torque as seen from the torque equation above. The armature rapidly accelerates producing a counter emf, which starts to reduce the motor current. Equilibrium is reached when the armature speed produces just the amount of counter emf required to limit motor current to the value needed in overcoming vehicle load and friction torques. If the driver lets up on the accelerator pedal, there is less applied voltage, less current flows in the field coils and in the armature. There is less torque, the armature slows, there is less back emf and equilibrium is again reached where the speed of the armature is sufficient to produce a back emf capable of limiting the motor current to the correct amount required to balance the new load and friction torques.

Figure 63 demonstrates characteristic curves of a series-wound dc motor. Notice how steeply the torque rises as current increases. Here one observes the operation of the "current squared" factor, derived in the torque equation. The speed of the motor would increase with no load if the series motor were not securely coupled to the drive shaft. This examples illustrates why belt

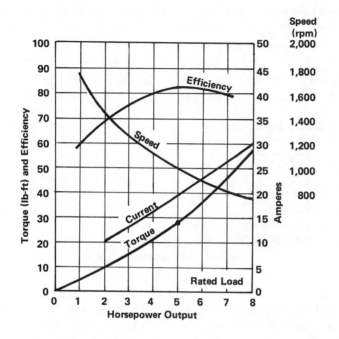

Figure 63. Characteristic curves of a series motor.
Courtesy: U.S. Navy Bureau of Personnel.

driven shafts do not have the inherent safety factor that gear-coupled motors possess. The efficiency of the motor peaks at full load, but maintains a high value over a wide range of its operating current. In urban driving particularly, where the load on the motor varies from moment to moment, one would use an integrated efficiency, as was done in the section on heating. Because of its attractive characteristics and simplicity, the series-wound dc motor is widely used as a torque source for electric vehicles.

SHUNT-WOUND DC MOTOR

A shunt-wound motor receives its name from the design which places its field coils in parallel or in shunt with the armature across the supply voltage. A shunt motor, like all large motors, on starting requires a controller to limit the inrush of current to the armature. The armature resistance is small, and because of the high moment of inertia of the rotor, the large current would have long duration before the rotor would gain sufficient speed to generate a back emf that would limit the current. The windings during that interval could be damaged. So a controller must be employed to limit starting current and control speed. As can be seen from the torque equation, the starting torque of a shunt motor will be less than for a series motor with given current.

$$T = k\phi I_a$$

Referring to Figure 64, observe that with a shunt motor, flux is independent of the armature current, while in a series motor it is directly related. The

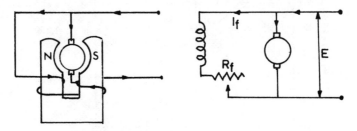

Figure 64. Shunt-excited machine.

shunt motor, like the compound motor, next to be discussed, can have two means of speed control: by varying the field current and thus the flux, and by lowering the voltage on the armature. This variation follows from the speed equation

$$rpm = \frac{(E_a - I_a R_a)}{k\phi}$$

If a resistance is introduced into the field winding, the current decreases, thus lowering the magnetic flux. Such an approach is illustrated in Figure 64. This action reduces the back emf of the motor, resulting in greater armature current, and increasing torque because the increase in armature current is much greater than the decrease in flux. The motor then speeds up until the back emf again is in balance. Field control on a shunt motor is for speeds greater than normal running speed. To reduce the speed of a shunt motor, one must decrease the voltage on the armature as seen from the speed equation. Figure 65 characterizes a shunt motor.

The shunt motor with these two speed controls can be varied in speed from zero up to the maximum speed for which the motor was designed. Thus the shunt motor, like the compound-wound motor, allowing for speed variation by permitting changes both in field current and in the armature current, can have more complex controls than are required for the series motor.

CUMULATIVE COMPOUND-WOUND DC MOTOR

Cumulative compound-wound dc motors (Figure 66) may also be used in electric vehicles. Like the series-wound dc motor, the compound has a high

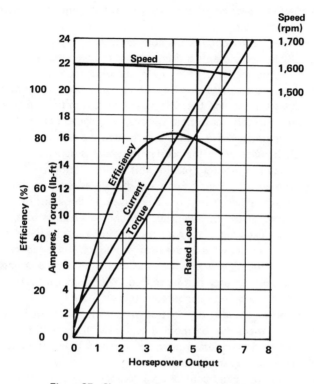

Figure 65. Characteristic curves of a shunt motor.
Courtesy: U.S. Navy Bureau of Personnel

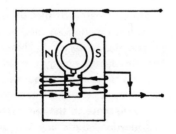

Figure 66. A cumulative compound-wound dc motor has shunt field coils supplementing the magnetic flux of the series field coils.

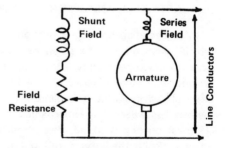

Figure 67. Diagram of a compound-wound dc motor with a variable resistance in the field winding. An increase of resistance reduces the field current which in turn decreases the magnetic flux. From the speed equation, this change results in an increase of the motor rpm.

starting torque; and because of the extra shunt windings, it can offer more flexibility in control than does the series motor. Compensating, however, is the fact that its control circuits are more complex. The type motor chosen to power a vehicle, therefore, is a decision that must be made by the manufacturer. As can be seen from Figure 67, cumulative compound-wound dc motors differ from the series-wound direct current motor. Each pole on the former has two windings, and the direction of current in the windings is such that the flux produced by both field windings supplement each other. In an operational examination of a cumulative compound-wound dc motor, the same approach is made when the accelerator pedal is depressed or let up as for the series wound motor. In making this analysis, knowing the action of the back emf and how it affects current and speed is essential.

Figure 67 illustrates speed control. The current in the shunt field windings of a compound motor can be independently controlled apart from the armature current. The speed of a compound motor can be substantially controlled by varying the current flowing in the field windings. If one reduces the current in the field, there is less magnetic flux being cut by the armature conductors. This means the back emf is reduced. With a smaller back emf, more current flows in the armature conductors, there is more force on the conductors, and the motor speeds up. Contrariwise, if more current is allowed to flow in the field, there will be more flux cut by the armature conductors, the back emf will rise, and less armature current will flow. There will be less force on the conductors, and as a consequence, less torque on the wheels, so the vehicle will slow. Field control on a compound motor can be used for speed control of a vehicle, in addition to the speed control applicable with voltage control on the armature.

REGENERATIVE AND DYNAMIC BRAKING

In regenerative braking, a portion of the kinetic energy of motion of a vehicle when brought to a halt or slowed is transformed from mechanical work to electrical energy and reintroduced into the battery. In dynamic braking, the same principle is employed, but the electric energy instead of being placed in a battery is dissipated as heat in a resistance. In both cases there is less wear on the mechanical braking surfaces. While the theory of electrical braking is sound, does it make economic sense to the automobile driver? While the jury is still out on this question, there can be some discussion.

In driving a vehicle, the pattern is never the same. But surely where there is much "tail gate" driving, regenerative braking has more merit than when the road is open. On the other hand, the best type motor for regenerative braking is a cumulative compound with provision for varying and strengthening the shunt field. To achieve regenerative braking satisfactorily, as the vehicle continually slows, the shunt field magnetic flux will need to be increased continually. This requires an additional control circuit. The increased energy introduced into the battery is probably about 2 to 8% of the amount consumed on the trip. Nearly every time the brake of the vehicle is applied there is a reverse flow of current into the battery. This action serves to restore the ion depletion balance which has typically become unbalanced in longer sustained driving. This charging current, though short, will encourage the sulfate ions to diffuse to the reaction sites, and additional energy may be obtained from the battery above that being reintroduced. There can be a negative factor, however. The current available to be reintroduced into the battery can readily be greater than the battery may accept without gassing. There can be control circuits, but these add a cost factor.

In saved energy, at 6000 miles per year about 3000 kwh would have been consumed at a cost of about $100. If the saving is 2 to 8%, the dollar saving would be $2 to $8 per year. If the electronics cost an extra $100, it has not been worthwhile. Of all the controversial elements that can be placed on an electric vehicle, regenerative braking is one of the most questionable.

CARE OF ELECTRIC MOTORS

An electric motor is one of the most reliable servants of man. They have been known to run for extended periods with only minimal attention. To secure the best operation of any motor, at regular intervals there should be a systematic inspection, depending, of course, on the service and operating conditions. Particular areas for examination would be: overall cleanliness, brushes, commutator, motor heating and bearings.

Cleanliness

As in any enterprise, good housekeeping leads to superior performance. So a motor, both interior and exterior, should be free of dirt, grease, oil and water. To remove loose material, a vacuum cleaner may be used. For adhering particles, a wiping rag can prove useful.

Brushes

Any motor manufacturer will relate that the heart of a dc motor is its ability to commutate successfully. In design and construction of a commutator, both science and art are involved. The purpose of the commutator is described in the introduction to electric motors. The motor brushes should have periodic inspections to confirm that they move freely in their holders. At the same time, the brushes must have secure and even contact on the commutator segments. The electric car dealer will want to possess extra brushes. On an electric car, there is growing indication that brush life will be a substantial number of years. When new brushes are installed they should be fitted with care to the commutator. Figure 68 shows a commutator and its brush housing.

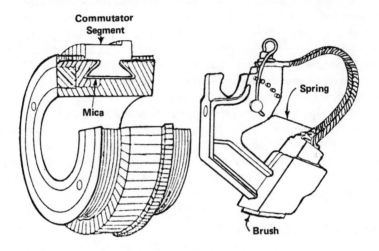

Figure 68. View of commutator and brush arrangement.
Courtesy: Theodore Audel & Co.

Commutator

A commutator surface should always have a polished appearance. Only infrequently will the commutator surface need wiping with a dry cloth. Place no oil on the commutator, since brushes available currently are of a graphite compound and are self-lubricating. For the service man, in case of brush chatter, a stethoscope effect may be obtained by placing the point of a wooden pencil on the exposed end of the brush. In case of chatter, vibrations will be sensed. In general, chatter will grow worse with time. The antidote is to use the surface smoothing tool shown in Figure 69. With proper application between brushes, and while the armature is slowly turned, the commutator surface is made concentric.

Heating

Insulation on current-carrying conductors is rated in quality and in temperature tolerance by letters in the alphabet. Class H insulation is better than class A. Class H insulation on a motor will enable it to be operated at

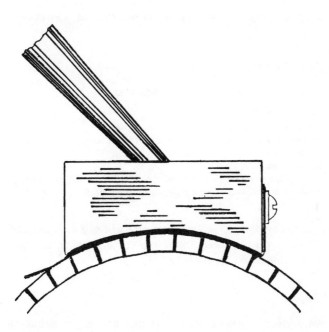

Figure 69. Showing method of sandpapering commutator. Sandpaper should be
attached to a block formed to the curvature of the commutator.
Courtesy: Theodore Audel & Co.

a temperature as high as 150°C, a temperature much too hot for the hand.
For accurate determination, a thermometer would need to be employed.
From time to time in any vehicle, after a long fast run has been made, the
body temperature of the motor should be felt. While the body is not the
warmest area, it provides a measure of the motor's heating.

Bearings

The manufacturer before shipping will place grease in the bearing housing.
If the motor has ball bearings there will usually be a pressure gun fitting.
When periodically inspected:

1. As with the motor, wipe clean the pressure gun fitting and the relief
   plug as well as the surrounding area.
2. Remove and clean the relief plug.
3. With the motor slowly turning, add grease until it emerges from the
   relief hole.
4. Run the motor for a short time with the relief hole open, expelling the
   excess grease. This action also serves to eject the old grease.
5. Replace the cleaned relief plug.

For bearing use, grease with the consistency of petroleum jelly is recommended.

General Observations

When troubleshooting a motor determine that:

1. The armature rotates freely.
2. The brush and brush holders are in good order.
3. The bearings are satisfactory and are well lubricated.
4. The air gap between rotor and stator is uniform.
5. All nuts and bolts are secure.
6. Fuses and contactors are clean and good electrical contacts are made.
7. There is a complete electrical circuit between battery, motor, and return to the battery.

As stated at the beginning, an electric motor will prove a good and faithful servant. Give it a little recognition from time to time, and you will be amazed at how fine it will perform.

CONCLUSIONS

A modern electric vehicle should be designed as an electromechanical system in which the mass of the vehicle, the battery system and its charger, the motor controls, the motor and its characteristics, the braking and lighting system of the vehicle are all balanced one with another. Further, because the electrical system can give long, trouble-free service, the body and chassis of an electric vehicle should be designed for long life.

Happily there is a growing realization among manufacturers of the need for this system approach. As a consequence, the user may expect to see constant improvement in electric vehicles. The consumer, therefore, will have at his disposal high-performance personal transportation dependably effective in its on-board use of electric energy. Finally, the best electric vehicles now available have characteristics which will be exceeded only well into the 1980s. The task now remaining is to place these superior electric vehicles on the streets of America and other countries where they will be seen. Their convenient, effectiveness, and economy will enable them to establish a position as an alternate means of personal transportation.

REFERENCES

1. Gross, Sidney. "Review of Candidate Batteries for Electrical Vehicles," *Energy Conversion* 15(3/4) (1976).

CHAPTER 4

ON-ROAD OPERATION OF ELECTRIC VEHICLES

"Have all the traffic lights on the streets turn red—and keep them that way."
George S. Kaufman's solution to the traffic problem in
New York City

HELPFUL HINTS FROM THE ROAD

In driving an electric vehicle, the operator soon learns a number of things that enable him to use his vehicle more effectively.

• With electric vehicles, it is good practice to charge the battery after every trip. Even a 15-minute charge is helpful. Not only does such current flow replenish the battery, but, in addition, it depolarizes the battery, lessens its internal resistance, and contributes to longer life. Suggestion: Always maintain the battery as fully charged as possible.

• When driving, observe the road farther ahead than you would with a gasoline-powered vehicle. Time your speed to pass through traffic lights without stopping. Avoid rapid acceleration, except where definitely needed. Such operation will extend the vehicle's range.

• Coast your vehicle where possible rather than use the brakes. The energy flowing into the brake lining when stopping probably came from the battery.

• If, when driving, you run out of electric energy, pull over to the side of the road. In ten minutes the battery will have sufficiently depolarized to drive the vehicle a considerable distance. Drive slowly at this time on the shoulder.

• When a long trip needs to be made in an electric vehicle, cruise at 30 mph, and avoid stopping as much as possible.

ELECTRIC VEHICLES—WHAT TO DO IF. . .

1. If you are driving and your battery runs down?

Answer: Pull over to the curb or on the shoulder where it is safe to park. Wait ten minutes. Depolarization of the battery will occur. This period, allowing a chemical change to occur in the battery, will probably enable you to reach an electrical outlet. The longer the period of depolarization, the farther you can drive. When you plug in your charging cord, for every hour of charge you will be able to drive 3 to 5 miles. Now, it is in the nature of a battery to give about 10 to 15 miles of advance notice that the energy stored in the battery is depleted. Indications are: your top speed is reduced, and the car's acceleration is sluggish.

2. If you are driving and there is no longer motive power?

Answer: The electrical circuit has been interrupted. This circuit runs from the battery positive terminal, through the current interrupting device, the control circuit, the motor, and to the negative battery terminal. If the motive power batteries are depleted, the most likely fault is that the circuit breaker has opened. If instant pull-in of the relay on the circuit breaker is needed, tread repeatedly on the accelerator pedal. This generally actuates the relay. Waiting a short time for the battery to depolarize can be rewarding. But obtain a charge as soon as possible. That is the best antidote.

3. If you find your batteries are at a high temperature (hot to the touch)?

Answer: Check the water level. Batteries heat when charging. They heat when driving. Their temperature should be maintained lower than 120°F. Batteries cool on resting. If one drives 4000 miles per year, typical for electric vehicles, battery watering may be expected every 4 to 8 weeks, depending on the climate.

4. If you regularly find one (or more) cells require water far more often than the others?

Answer: There is a fault in that cell. Your batteries have probably been used for some time. All cells eventually fail. This initial battery failure is probably the beginning of successive failures over a period of time. A deficient cell is also indicated by reductions in your top speed, and in more sluggish acceleration. If the batteries are of relatively recent purchase, either replace the bad battery with a new one or with one which a reputable garage man indicates accepts a charge satisfactorily. Mark the battery newly inserted and keep an eye on it.

5. If your battery terminals are corroded with a gray-green coating?

Answer: Realize that a battery voltage can be *lethal.* Operate with care. A skilled mechanic should carefully remove the cable from the battery terminal utilizing an insulated wrench. With an insulated handled brush, vigorously remove the corrosion. With terminals and cable connection cleaned, spray the surfaces with Zappon, then reconnect.

6. If there is a chattering noise from the armature of the motor?
Answer: Such a sound will best be heard if the accelerator pedal is carefully depressed with the transmission not in gear. Then with the hood up, a second observer can listen as the pedal is pressed slowly up and down. If the chatter depends on the speed of the motor, the sound is due to brush chatter. In all probability this repair can be made by a mechanic holding a special commutator bar file against the commutator bar surfaces while the car motor slowly turns. With care the chatter will be eliminated.

7. If a constant or almost constant squeak is heard issuing from under the hood?
Answer: Grease is required at a bearing surface. The motor has but two places containing bearings—at the front and back end of the motor. (Refer to the section on care of the motor.) Listen also to the bearings on the alternator, if such a device is present on the car.

8. If you are driving and hit a puddle so deep that water gets inside the motor?
Answer: Remove the motor from the water as soon as possible. Drive the car to a garage. Relate your experience to the mechanic. The motor may require removal, cleaning and drying by heat.

9. If you are driving and are told that smoke comes from the battery compartment?
Answer: At least one cell is almost surely out of water. See question 4.

10. If on acceleration you hear water squirting from the cell breather orifice?
Answer: If the batteries are new and in good order, there may be too much electrolyte in the battery. Heating the battery squeezes out the excess. If the battery set is old, almost surely there is a poor cell. With such a cell, there might be an internal resistance. On acceleration of the car, the heavy current reacting with this cell resistance liberates heat, boiling the water. The generated steam forces the excess electrolyte out of the orifice. Replace that battery. Repetitive emission from the breather orifice will discolor the top of the offending battery. See question 4.

11. If when driving the motive power is repeatedly interrupted and the vehicle stops and then starts again in a short time?
Answer: The batteries are probably near the end of life, and the battery voltage is low. Such characteristics allow the circuit breaker to open repeatedly, causing arcing and possible damage not only to that contact surface, but to the silicon control rectifiers as well. Insert a new set of batteries.

12. If you attempt to charge the batteries and the ammeter on the charger reads zero even though you have turned on the switch?

Answer: Only a technician should execute the following. If the charger does not hum, no current is reaching the charger transformer. Determine if there is voltage available at the receptacle where your line cord is plugged. If such a voltage is present, detach the charging cord plug, isolating the charger. A skilled mechanic can determine if a fuse in the charger is good with the aid of an ohmmeter. If voltage is shown to be on the charger side of the fuse, with still no current to the battery, have your mechanic disconnect the charger plug on the battery side of the charger. Determine if voltage is at this point. If it is, disconnect the balance of the circuit. Trace the circuit through for continuity. If there is no voltage at the charger outlet, even though the fuse is good, the fault is in the charger. Replace the charger.

13. If you inspect the batteries for water level and in some cells there are small clouds of vapor being emitted when the caps are removed?

Answer: The battery with the emitting clouds is operating at a higher temperature than the others. Inspect the water level. The higher temperature is an indication of probable early failure of this battery.

14. If you are on the road and seeking a 115-volt receptacle, and the receptacle does not fit your charging cord plug?

Answer: There are numerous configurations for 115-volt receptacles. Your vehicle has been provided with the most common. If you have the *Handy Kit*, determine if one of those provided fits. If not, proceed to another location where a receptacle matches your plug.

15. If the car has run over the charging cable and bent the plug pins?

Answer: Safety would indicate a new charging cable connector should be installed. The chance of damage inside the plug is great.

CHAPTER 5

NOVEL IDEAS FROM THE ROAD

"The rapid progress true science now makes, occasions my regretting sometimes that I was born so soon. It is impossible to imagine the height to which may be carried, in a thousand years, the power of man over matter."

Benjamin Franklin to Joseph Priestley,
February 8, 1780

Any person long around electric vehicles either as a driver, or as a designer, receives many suggestions. To the author of this book, the generosity of the average American with an idea is truly awe-inspiring. The loquaciousness of the onlooker may be associated with the inherent freedom of expression of Americans, or the inner belief of many that they can make an improvement in an electric vehicle. The free giving of advice may be a national trait. It may be that foreign nationals are more taciturn not only in "street talk," but in university research, family matters, and the general activities of life.

Following are a number of novel and fanciful ideas that have been presented to the author of this book concerning electric vehicles. The serious engineer developing electric cars is a target for many concepts related to their design. Included are several line drawings which serve to demonstrate principles which a vehicle designer hears many times. While few of the ideas unceremoniously related have merit, there is no reason why a person should not dream. Included in the following pages are various schemes embodying perpetual motion, the utilization of solar energy, applying the power of the wind, the application of rolling resistance to enhance motive power, the use of laser power, and other plans even more obscure. As the careful reader will discover, in range, cost and convenience, it is difficult to improve upon the storage battery when considering alternatives of energy storage for an electric vehicle.

SAIL AND WIND POWER

Perpetual motion! How that idea persists in the minds of those who approach me with ideas for electric vehicles. Variations of this concept are received from all classes of people, but seldom if ever from the science-trained university graduate.

The car with a sail (Figure 70) is a concept which has been frequently presented. Yet the person who offers this suggestion will himself, on the open highway, drive 60 mph and probably never in his life has stood up to a wind of like velocity. Can the person who makes such a suggestion fail to realize the power required to move a vehicle? Surely he has had the experience of trying to shove one on the pavement, a task which is possible for a sub-compact car, but for a full-sized sedan essentially cannot be done. If one refers to cruising power in Figure 13A, 60 hp is required to move a 6000-pound van 60 mph. For a cruising speed of 30 mph, 12 horsepower is required. These are power requirements vastly in excess of the pulling power of a sail, except in full gale conditions. And then the breeze may not be in a favorable direction—a fact appreciated by our forefathers who sailed commerce from port to port. One would conclude, therefore, that sails on a land vehicle should be considered only for the rare, lightweight sport vehicle.

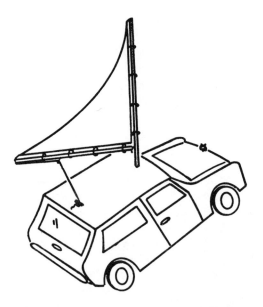

Figure 70. With a strong tail wind, hoist your sail and save your batteries.
The *Christian Science Monitor* of October 15, 1976, describes a more sophisticated
sail vehicle equipped with an electric drive system.

AIRPLANE WING ON ELECTRIC VEHICLES

A northern California initiate to electric vehicles suggested he has bank funding to provide an electric vehicle bearing an airplane wing raised vertically as shown in Figure 71. He claims its high aspect ratio would permit him not only to travel with the wind, but, most importantly, sail close to the direction from which the wind arises. Like the man with the canvas sail on his dream vehicle, this innovator failed to realize the power required to move a vehicle.

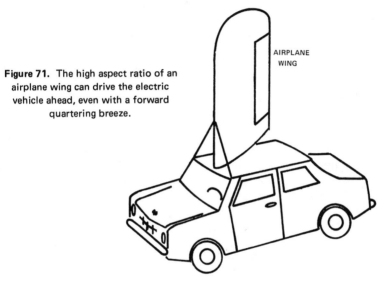

AIRPLANE WING

Figure 71. The high aspect ratio of an airplane wing can drive the electric vehicle ahead, even with a forward quartering breeze.

WIND-DRIVEN FAN ELECTRIC VEHICLE

The wind-driven fan electric vehicle idea emerges periodically in various forms. The crudest representation is the vehicle carrying a windmill on its roof. In a more sophisticated version, the wind-driven turbine is placed where the radiator is located on an internal combustion vehicle. The blades drive a shaft on which a generator is mounted. Forward motion of the vehicle provides movement of air over the rotor blades, contributing to the shaft's rotation and the generation of electricity (see Figure 72).

That version of the wind-driven fan on top of the vehicle is universally bad. The more compact version in front of the vehicle principally adds cost to the vehicle. Figure 73 illustrates this principle.

Igra[1] has done work on a wind generator which conceivably could be placed on a car. Such a power source he calls a shrouded aerogenerator. He points out that wind has a low energy content because of its low density,

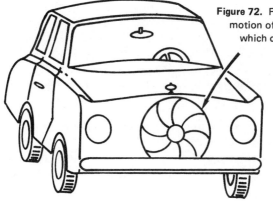

Figure 72. Fan, actuated by forward motion of car, drives generator which charges car battery.

being approximately one-thousandth that of water. He states that the maximum available energy from an ideal windmill is 59.3% of the stream-tube that covers the windmill blades. Power generated is at a maximum when the velocity of the wind out of the rotor is one-third of the upwind velocity. Real efficiency will be less due to aerodynamic and mechanical losses. He found 6 to 8 blade rotors most efficient. Golding[2] covers many more factors including numerous types of wind generators. Finally, the *Encyclopaedia Britannica*[3] gives a rule of thumb for power in the wind equation

$$kw = 4 \times D^2 \times V^3 \times 10^{-6}$$

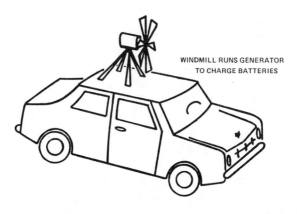

WINDMILL RUNS GENERATOR
TO CHARGE BATTERIES

Figure 73. Wind-powered electric car.

where diameter of the windmill is in feet and V is wind velocity in miles per hour. The encyclopedia account further states that about 5% of the flow-through wind energy is converted into electrical energy. The question is how much increased distance will be obtained if a wind generator is on the car, based on the range of the vehicle. Assume the blades have a diameter of one foot. Assume the average urban driving speed is 20 mph. Assume the car requires 0.3 kwh per mile. Assume the urban driving range is 70 miles. Therefore, driving time to complete range is 3½ hours.

$$kwh = 4 \times D^2 \times V^3 \times 10^{-6} \times \text{efficiency} \times \text{driving time}$$
$$= 4 \times 1^2 \times 20^3 \times 10^{-6} \times 0.05 \times 3\frac{1}{2} \text{ hours}$$
$$= 5.6 \text{ watt-hours (w-h)}$$

If $\qquad$ 0.3 kwh = 300 w-h = 1 mile = 5280 feet
$$1 \text{ w-h} = 5280/300$$
$$= 17 \text{ feet}$$

Then $\qquad$ 5.6 w-h = 95 feet.

In 70 miles increased distance achieved by having a wind generator on the car is 95 feet. The important observation is not that it is 95 feet, but that even if the results were off by a factor of ten, the increase is essentially negligible.

Figure 74. Replaceable batteries on an interchange basis at service stations could increase the range of the electric car.

SOLAR POWER ON ELECTRIC VEHICLES

Solar power[4] is a phrase now in common usage. It offers the twin claims of age-old respectability, and the patina of being free. To use this God-given source of energy, the comment is often made of equipping a roof of a vehicle with photocells. While substantial effort is presently being made to lower the purchase price of electric vehicles, the use of solar cells would add greatly to their cost and would provide little power either to the motor or the battery. Figure 75 illustrates such a car.

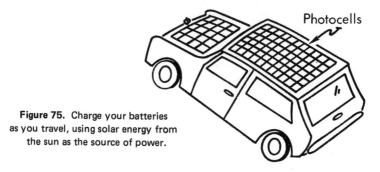

Photocells

Figure 75. Charge your batteries as you travel, using solar energy from the sun as the source of power.

When the sun's rays are vertical, about 1 kilowatt of power impinges on 1 square yard. If photocells were placed on the roof and hood of the car as shown, possibly 2 kilowatts of power would be received at midday. At best, when new, these photocells have an efficiency of perhaps 18%,* resulting in 360 watts of useful electric power. Such a two-square-yard surface exposed for 1 hour, assuming 100% storage efficiency and 100% efficiency of transferring electric energy into mechanical energy, a 6000-pound van would be moved only 1 mile at 30 mph. In the real world of efficiencies, knowing the difficulty of converting the low voltage of the solar cell to the high voltage required by the energy storage system, the loss in efficiency in electric controls, in the motor, and in mechanical linkages, possibly less than 5% of the 1 mile would be realized at 30 mph. Five percent of 1 mile is 210 feet. That would be the extra distance the van could be driven after one hour's exposure to sunshine. Solar cells do not, at this stage of their development, offer a fruitful source of energy for electric vehicles. Space science, however, where photocells have proved effective, has raised the expectations of Americans. But applied to moving over-the-road vehicles, solar cells leave much to be desired in energy collection, cost, and moving an electric vehicle.

*In 1976 nonspace voltaic cells are quoted at $20,000 per kilowatt versus $600 per peak kilowatt for a conventional steam electric generating plant. The latter can generate electricity day and night. It is interesting to note that the efficiency of a photovoltaic cell is about the same as the efficiency of a gasoline-fueled engine.

SOLAR-STIMULATED FLUCTUATING-VOLTAGE
ELECTRIC GENERATOR

With a name inversely as long as the device is small, another theoretical means of utilizing solar energy to create electric energy has been suggested by Joseph C. Yates of the Innovative Center of the Massachusetts Institute of Technology.[5] His conversion device is a microcircuit sandwich element consisting of a flat-surface resistor which is heated by the sun. Random electron motion from solar heating provides a minute oscillating voltage across a capacitor spanning a thermal barrier, such as a vacuum. Diodes on the cool side change the resulting oscillating voltage and current into direct current. Current flow from millions of these tiny microcircuits is channeled into a common electrial circuit which provides useful dc current to charge a battery, heat a home, or, conceivably to operate a dc motor of an electric vehicle. Yates claims he will obtain an efficiency of 80%, an efficiency five times greater than that from a presently obtainable photocell. The vacuum thermal barrier he thinks is the "big step." If the system works, Yates can visualize in 5 to 10 years the development of solar electric generators from a "fully automated microfabrication technique, utilizing X-ray lithography to reproduce the circuits " (see Figure 76).

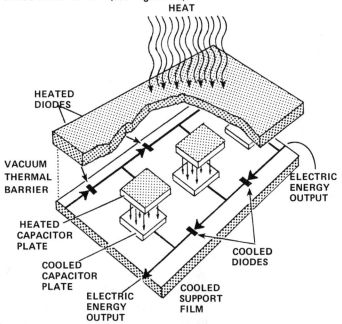

Figure 76. Power conversion circuit (in expanded isometric). Electricity is created when sun heats resistor, top layer, and generates voltage. Second layer, capacitor, transfers it across vacuum, and third, diode, converts it into direct current.
Courtesy: *Los Angeles Times.*

With two square meters of Yates' microcircuits on the roof of an automobile, about 1.5 kw of power would be generated, barely sufficient to accelerate slowly only the very lightest of cars. After a one-hour charging of a GameTime 120 type vehicle, it might travel a mile. The cost of Yates' Solar-Stimulated Fluctuating-Voltage Electric Generator in quantity has not been stated.

ON-BOARD GENERATION OF ELECTRICAL ENERGY

Surely the most frequent suggestion I receive to enhance the range of an electric vehicle is a type of perpetual motion concept shown in Figure 77.

Figure 77. Gear on rear wheel with chain connection to dc generator. Output from generator charges battery as the vehicle moves forward. Here is an example of "perpetual motion."

Interestingly enough, in our successfully marketed vehicles, we use a segment of this principle, and with remarkable success. Rather than having the battery charged by a generator chain-connected to the wheels, we use a belt to transfer power from the motor drive shaft to turn a small ac generator, an alternator, to charge through a rectifier, changing the ac to dc power, then feeding the 12-volt battery in the electric vehicle. This auxiliary battery serves to supply energy to the lights, horn, windshield wiper, etc., all of which are electrically operated.

In suggesting a generator to charge the motive-power battery, the would-be innovator overlooks an important fact. To generate electric energy by the means described here requires the input of mechanical energy, and in an amount greater than the electrical energy which results. As effectively as the human body is capable of working, for example in riding a bicycle at full speed, if all that energy were placed in an electric generator, you could light only a 100-watt lamp, and then only during the time all of your physical energy was being expended. Reduce your effort a small amount, and the lamp would noticeably dim.

A variation of this self-generation principle can be used to equip an electric vehicle with the necessary control circuit, so that when the brake pedal is actuated, the motor is automatically modified from a consumer of power to a generator; and the power generated can be made to flow into the battery. In this case the kinetic energy of the moving vehicle, as it slows, is transformed into electric power, which is stored in the battery.

While this principle, known as regenerative braking, could be used on a passenger electric vehicle, giving an additional 5% range in typical urban use, on an economic basis its employment is difficult to justify. An example will bear out this assertion. Suppose the installation of a regenerative braking system on your electric vehicle, as an option, costs $150. Suppose further that the range of the electric vehicle with regenerative braking is enhanced 5%, or 3 to 4 miles; that a modern full-size electric vehicle travels 2 miles on 4¢ worth of electricity; and that the electric vehicle covers 40 miles per day. Such a distance yields an electric energy cost of about 80¢. If one drives the vehicle 40 miles per day (high, on the average) for 250 days in the year, the energy cost of travel would be $200. But with regenerative braking 5% was saved, or $10. Yet this energy option cost $150. Thus, in the case illustrated, regenerative braking would have a 15-year payout with no interest cost, and a 25- or 30-year payout including the cost of the money. So, good energy-saving principles must always be investigated before adaption for general use.

There are other factors concerning regenerative braking which go beyond the scope of this book. For example, a shunt or compound motor is more suitable for regenerative braking than is a series motor, yet a series motor is attractive for its high initial torque, which in certain cases can obviate the use of a transmission. And a transmission consumes 6% of its throughput power, as well as having a first cost. Also, is that extra 5% range, possibly available with regenerative braking, important? Another factor has to do with batteries. With regenerative braking applied, current flow through the battery is reversed. This action depolarizes the battery, and possibly adds to its life. How important is such an observation? Still another consideration, a noneconomic one: Is regenerative braking a prestige accessory? Such egobuilding devices can be very important to the possessor. For these and other reasons the use of regenerative braking is controversial. But all agree that to an electric vehicle it adds complexity and contributes to still greater first cost.

EXTENSION CORD VEHICLES

Since electric lawnmowers are operated from extension cords, all who work with electric vehicles are jestingly given the concept of the automobile with the long extension cord. Figure 78 illustrates such a principle. It is a

Figure 78. Electric car with long extension cord.

serious possibility that a large vehicle can be satisfactorily served by an umbilical connection at various locations. An example: construction site vehicles, that go back and forth alongside the facade of a building, providing supplies to construction stations.

THE STEAM WANKEL INTERMEDIARY LINK

The brother of a salesman who works for a dealer marketing our electric vehicles, presented me with the following idea for an electric vehicle. The principle of operation can best be appreciated by viewing Figure 79. Energy from a large battery heats water in a boiler, generating steam. This steam passes through a Wankel engine, which is belt-coupled to an electric generator. Power from this source is supplied to the electric motor, which provides torque to the wheels. The question I ask: Why not have the battery provide power to the traction motor directly? There is less hardware to carry.

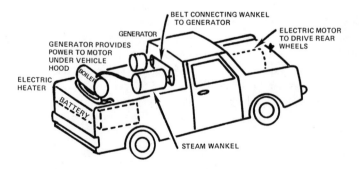

Figure 79. Battery supplies energy to heater under boiler. Steam from boiler is supplied to Wankel engine which in turn drives dc generator with a belt. Generator supplies power to drive electric motor for rear wheels.

FLYWHEEL ENERGY STORAGE

The Swiss Oerlikon Gyrobus was a vehicle powered from the energy stored in a flywheel which weighed 3300 pounds.[6] Energy from this rotating source propelled a 70-passenger bus between stops separated an average of ¾ mile. At such times an electric contact was made with an overhead trolley and the flywheel was again brought up to speed by action of an electric motor. But the passengers became impatient with the need for frequent respinning of the rotating mass, so the bus was retired in 1969. This flywheel would run only 4½ hours from full speed to standstill without load. Even in a reduced atmosphere it coasted only 12 hours.

While the above was not a particularly successful operation, flywheels do have attractive possibilities. They can be brought up to speed as quickly as the electrical system can supply energy, drain rates can be as high as 5000 watts per pound compared to 50 watts per pound for lead-acid batteries, cycle life is estimated to be over 100,000 times as compared to the lead-acid battery of 500 to 1000 times; they are highly efficient in delivery of power; and it has been calculated that if losses due to the magnetic bearing were eliminated, in coasting it would take a flywheel 10 years to reach 37% of its initial speed.[7] One system is illustrated in Figure 80.

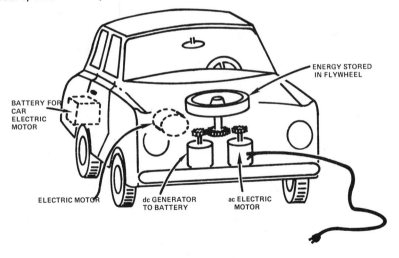

Figure 80. An ac operated electric motor spins the flywheel. The flywheel stores kinetic energy. The gear from the ac motor, through transfer, engages the dc generator which in turn charges the motive-power battery. The ac plug is disconnected from its receptacle when battery has become charged. As the electric motor for car discharges the battery, kinetic energy from the flywheel drives the dc generator which charges the battery, thus supplying electricity to the car motor. The car starts on its trip with energy stored both electrically and mechanically.

Richard and Stephen Post, father and son, treat[8] energy storage in fly-wheels. They comment that while flywheels have been traditionally made of steel, fiber composites initially developed for aerospace needs have far more desirable qualities. As they state, "The limiting amount of energy that can be stored per unit weight of flywheel material is equal to half the tensile strength at the breaking point, divided by the density." The Posts show that a fused silica flywheel, under ideal conditions, could store as much as 870 watt-hours per kilogram as compared to 20 to 30 watt-hours for lead-acid batteries.

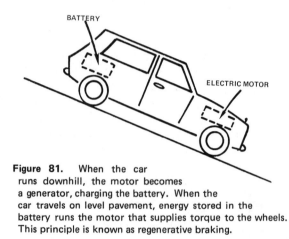

Figure 81. When the car runs downhill, the motor becomes a generator, charging the battery. When the car travels on level pavement, energy stored in the battery runs the motor that supplies torque to the wheels. This principle is known as regenerative braking.

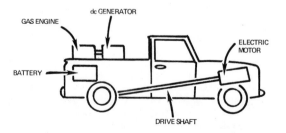

Figure 82. A gasoline motor-generator set provides dc power to the batteries, which in turn allows the electric motor to turn the rear wheels.

Figure 83. A gasoline motor and dc generator in the trailer constantly charge the car batteries. The batteries in turn supply energy to the electric motor. The motor provides torque to the wheels. One such vehicle traveled from Detroit to Washington with only convenience stops.

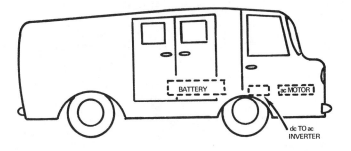

Figure 84. Direct current from battery is supplied an inverter which changes dc power to three-phase ac power, with frequency control. Squirrel-cage induction motor supplies torque to the wheels. A number of high-performance vehicles have been built using this technique. The method provides an elegant, sophisticated electric drive system, but is now too expensive for the power requirements of vehicles here considered.

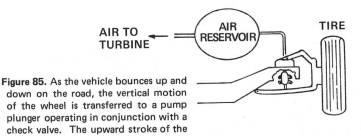

Figure 85. As the vehicle bounces up and down on the road, the vertical motion of the wheel is transferred to a pump plunger operating in conjunction with a check valve. The upward stroke of the piston places additional air in the air reservoir. A spring withdraws the piston for the next upward thrust. As the air flows from the container, it passes over the vanes of a turbine. This turbine drives a generator to charge the battery. A pump, thus operating, is located at each wheel, feeding air to a common reservoir. (U.S. Patent 3,507,580, Filed May 12, 1967.)

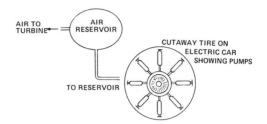

Figure 86. As the vehicle wheel moves over the pavement, the tire flattens slightly at its contact with the road. Pumps, shown within the tire, have their plungers driven upward as the piston-actuating rod is driven upward by the tire flattening. The pressure generated is given to a circulating fluid, such as air, and placed in a reservoir under pressure. Air then flows out of the reservoir under pressure to the vanes of a turbine. This turbine drives a generator and thus recharges the battery as the vehicle moves forward.

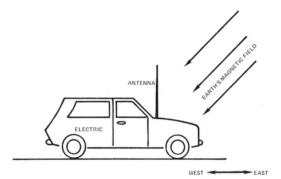

Figure 87. Since electricity can be generated by a wire cutting a magnetic field, equip the electric car with an antenna for cutting the earth's magnetic field. Feed the electricity generated to the motor which, in turn, drives the wheels. The earth's magnetic field runs from the North Magnetic Pole to the South Magnetic Pole, and power for the motor comes from the battery when the vehicle travels either north or south.

Figure 88. Laser beam power from an electric utility is collected by a parabolic antenna and stored in a small battery. An electric motor drives the wheels from energy supplied by the laser beam. When no beam is present, as in the "shade" of a building, power from the motor comes from the battery. An alternate method is to have power from the laser beam operate a motor which stores energy in a flywheel. Power from the flywheel is coupled to the drive wheels, either by way of a belt drive, or by an electric generator and then an electric motor.

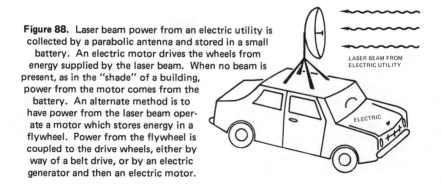

REFERENCES

1. Igra, O. "Design and Performance of a Turbine Suitable for an Aero-generator," *Energy Conversion* 15:143-151, Pergamon Press (1976).
2. Golding, E. W. *The Generation of Electricity by Windpower* (London: Spon, 1955).
3. *Encyclopaedia Brittanica*, Volume 23, pp. 655-656 (Chicago, 1959).
4. Chalmers, Bruce. "The Photovoltaic Generation of Electricity," *Scientific American* 235(4) (October 1976).
5. Kendall, John. *Los Angeles Times*, September 13, 1976, Part II, p. 1.
6. Weber, Richard and Sherwood B. Menkes. "Flywheel Energy Propulsion and the Electric Vehicle," *Third International Electric Vehicle Symposium,* Washington (1974).
7. Edgar, R. F. *et al.* "Magnetic Bearings for Aerospace Applications," TDR #63-474, Wright-Patterson Air Force Base, Ohio (1963).
8. Post, R. F. and S. F. Post. "Flywheels," *Scientific American* 229:6 (December 1973).

APPENDIX A

SYMBOLS AND SUPPLIES

The presence of this appendix indicates that electrical vehicles have progressed from the research and development stage, through the period of testing, and onto the streets into the hands of owners. To those long participating, this has been a tortuous and often frustrating experience. The symbolic white mountain that each must climb in life to achieve fulfillment has had, in the case of electric vehicles, almost unscalable approaches. These difficulties may be explained chiefly by the fact that internal combustion vehicles are highly developed, well-made, economically priced, and offer a universal web of service facilities. The growing recognition by the American public of the finite limit of petroleum products, the increasing general awareness of air pollution, and the recent long lines at gasoline pumps have all been positive forces for alternate vehicle drive systems. Inasmuch as this volume is about electric vehicles, the symbols applicable to this class of vehicle have been assembled below. When applicable, the American National Standard Symbol has been used.

Just as the owner who wishes to look under the hood of an electric car may wish to know the symbols, so might he want a selection of tools, and want to be acquainted with the equipment and supplies for servicing electric vehicles. With this knowledge the owner himself can better judge the nature of a vehicle's ills. Finally a Handy Kit has been suggested and assembled particularly for the electric vehicle owner, containing an assortment of tools and material new owners will find useful.

125

SYMBOLS APPLICABLE TO ELECTRIC VEHICLES

Alternating current generator

Ammeter

Battery

Capacitor

Cumulative compound-wound
    dc motor

Diode

Inductance

Magnetic contactor

Receptacle, consumer vehicles

Receptacle, heavy vehicles

Resistance

Series-wound dc motor

Silicon control rectifier (SCR)

Transformer with core

Transistor, high-power junction

Voltmeter

Shunt-wound dc motor

ELECTRIC VEHICLE RELEVANT CONVERSIONS

1 British thermal unit (Btu) is the quantity of heat to raise one pound of water one degree Fahrenheit
1 gallon of gasoline on combustion yields 127,600 Btu
1 kilowatt-hour = 3413 Btu
1 gallon of gasoline contains the same energy as 37.4 kilowatt-hours

SPECIAL TOOLS, EQUIPMENT AND SUPPLIES
FOR SERVICING ELECTRIC MOTORS

Specific Electrical Equipment

Ammeter
Handy Kit, useful tool box specifically equipped for electric vehicles
Shunts
Voltmeter-Ohmmeter

The Battery Charger

Diodes (specify information inscribed on diode)
Fuses (specify current, type and manufacturer)

Motive Power and Lighting Batteries

Battery (specify ampere-hour and manufacturer)
Battery lifting slings
Cabling (specify vehicle)
Insulated wrenches
Lugs (specify type terminals)
Lug clamper
Zappon solution—for minimizing terminal corrosion

Circuit Breaker

Circuit breaker (specify manufacturer)

Control System

Controller (specify manufacturer)

Electric Motor

Brushes (specify size)
Commutator surface smoother

AMMETER—An instrument for measuring the amount of electron flow in amperes.

AMPERE—The basic unit of electrical current.

AMPERE-TURN—The magnetizing force produced by a current of one ampere flowing through a coil of one turn.

AMPLITUDE—The maximum instantaneous value of an alternating voltage or current measured in either the positive or negative direction.

ARC—A flash caused by an electric current ionizing a gas or vapor.

ARMATURE—The rotating part of an electric motor or generator. The moving part of a relay or vibrator.

ATTENUATOR—A network of resistors used to reduce voltage, current, or power delivered to a load.

BATTERY—Two or more primary or secondary cells connected together electrically. The term does not apply to a single cell.

BREAKER POINTS—Metal contacts that open and close a circuit at timed intervals.

BRUSH—The conducting material, usually a block of carbon, bearing against the commutator or slip rings through which the current flows in or out.

CAPACITOR—Two electrodes or sets of electrodes in the form of plates, separated from each other by an insulating material called the dielectric.

CIRCUIT—The complete path of an electric current.

CIRCUIT BREAKER—An electromagnetic or thermal device that opens a circuit when the current in the circuit exceeds a predetermined amount. Circuit breakers can be reset.

COMMUTATOR—The copper segments on the armature of a motor or generator. It is cylindrical in shape and is used to pass power into or from the brushes. It is a switching device.

CONDUCTANCE—The ability of a material to conduct or carry an electric current. It is the reciprocal of the resistance of the material, and is expressed in mhos.

CONDUCTIVITY—The ease with which a substance transmits electricity.

CONDUCTOR—Any material suitable for carrying electric current.

CORE—A magnetic material that affords an easy path for magnetic flux lines in a coil.

COUNTER EMF—Counter electromotive force; an emf induced in a coil or armature that opposes the applied voltage.

CYCLE—One complete positive and one complete negative alternation of a current or voltage.

129

DIELECTRIC—An insulator; a term that refers to the insulating material between the plates of a capacitor.

DIODE—Vacuum tube—a two element tube that contains a cathode and plate; semiconductor—a material of either germanium or silicon that is manufactured to allow current to flow in only one direction. Diodes are used as rectifiers and detectors.

DIRECT CURRENT—An electric current that flows in one direction only.

EDDY CURRENT—Induced circulating currents in a conducting material that are caused by a varying magnetic field.

EFFICIENCY—The ratio of output power to input power, generally expressed as a percentage.

ELECTROLYTE—A solution of a substance which is capable of conducting electricity. An electrolyte may be in the form of either a liquid or a paste.

ELECTROMAGNET—A magnet made by passing current through a coil of wire wound on a soft iron core.

ELECTROMOTIVE FORCE (emf)—The force that produces an electric current in a circuit.

ELECTRON—A negatively charged particle of matter.

ENERGY—The ability or capacity to do work.

FARAD—The unit of capacitance.

FIELD—The space containing electric or magnetic lines of force.

FIELD WINDING—The coil used to provide the magnetizing force in motors and generators.

FLUX FIELD—All electric or magnetic lines of force in a given region.

FREQUENCY—The number of complete cycles per second existing in any form of wave motion; such as the number of cycles per second of an alternating current.

FULL-WAVE RECTIFIER CIRCUIT—A circuit which utilizes both the positive and the negative alternations of an alternating current to produce a direct current.

FUSE—A protective device inserted in series with a circuit. It contains a metal that will melt or break when current is increased beyond a specific value for a definite period of time.

GALVANOMETER—An instrument used to measure small dc currents.

GENERATOR—A machine that converts mechanical energy into electrical energy.

GROUND—A metallic connection with the earth to establish ground potential. Also, a common return to a point of zero potential.

HERTZ—A unit of frequency equal to one cycle per second.

HENRY—The basic unit of inductance.

HORSEPOWER—The English unit of power, equal to work done at the rate of 550 foot-pounds per second. Equal to 746 watts of electrical power.

HYSTERESIS—A lagging of the magnetic flux in a magnetic material behind the magnetizing force which is producing it.

IMPEDANCE—The total opposition offered to the flow of an alternating current. It may consist of any combination of resistance, inductive reactance, and capacitive reactance.

INDUCTANCE—The property of a circuit which tends to oppose a change in the existing current.

INDUCTION—The act or process of producing voltage by the relative motion of a magnetic field across a conductor.

INDUCTIVE REACTANCE—The opposition to the flow of alternating or pulsating current caused by the inductance of a circuit. It is measured in ohms.

LINE OF FORCE—A line in an electric or magnetic field that shows the direction of the force.

LOAD—The power that is being delivered by any power-producing device. The equipment that uses the power from the power-producing device.

MAGNETIC FIELD—The space in which a magnetic force exists.

MAGNETIC FLUX—The total number of lines of force issuing from a pole of a magnet.

MUTUAL INDUCTANCE—A circuit property existing when the relative position of two inductors causes the magnetic lines of force from one to link with the turns of the other.

OHM—The unit of electrical resistance.

OHMMETER—An instrument for directly measuring resistance in ohms.

POLARITY—The character of having magnetic poles, or electric charges.

POLE—The section of a magnet where the flux lines are concentrated; also where they enter and leave the magnet. An electrode of a battery.

POTENTIAL—The amount of charge held by a body as compared to another point or body. Usually measured in volts.

POWER—The rate of doing work or the rate of expending energy. The unit of electrical power is the watt.

REACTANCE—The opposition offered to the flow of an alternating current by the inductance, capacitance, or both, in any circuit.

RESISTANCE—The opposition to the flow of current caused by the nature and physical dimensions of a conductor.

RESISTOR—A circuit element whose chief characteristic is resistance; used to oppose the flow of current.

SERIES-WOUND—A motor or generator in which the armature is wired in series with the field winding.

SOLENOID—An electromagnetic coil that contains a movable plunger.

TORQUE—The turning effort or twist which a shaft sustains when transmitting power.

TRANSFORMER—A device composed of two or more coils, linked by magnetic lines of force, used to transfer energy from one circuit to another.

VOLT—The unit of electrical potential.

VOLTMETER—An instrument designed to measure a difference in electrical potential, in volts.

WATT—The unit of electrical power.

WATTMETER—An instrument for measuring electrical power in watts.